ABC's
Of
Lighthearted Living
...My Rx

**Learn how Happy leads to Healthy.
Trust your Self. Love your Life.**

Margaret Mears md

Margaret Mears, M.D.

Outskirts Press, Inc.
Denver, Colorado

The opinions expressed in this manuscript are solely the opinions of the author and do not represent the opinions or thoughts of the publisher. The author represents and warrants that s/he either owns or has the legal right to publish all material in this book.

ABC's of Lighthearted Living...My Rx
Learn how Happy leads to Healthy. Trust your Self. Love your Life.
Copyright © 2008 Margaret Mears, M.D.
Graphics by Kate Blue, bluelizarddesigns@comcast.net
V4.0

Outskirts Press, Inc.
http://www.outskirtspress.com

ISBN: 978-1-4327-2480-1

Outskirts Press and the "OP" logo are trademarks belonging to Outskirts Press, Inc.

PRINTED IN THE UNITED STATES OF AMERICA

A Gift

To:

From:

Dedication

To my late husband, Ron, for all we shared.
You loved and laughed with me right to the end.

To Kelly, Kimberly, Jeff, Sandra and Randi,
and your beautiful children. Your light brightens our world.

Acknowledgments

My heartfelt thanks to all those friends, patients and family who shared and demonstrated their courage and lighthearted attitude over the past many years.

Thanks to Joan Domning for your wise editing; Rosanne Longo for your encouraging cheerful feedback while formatting; Natasha Quick, my publisher representative, for your patience in answering my seemingly endless stream of questions; to my friends and students who cheered me on, no matter what; and especially to Kate Blue, who created the amazing graphics for this work. I told you what I wanted, and you let your outstanding talent go to work. The alphabet creatures are at once whimsical, delightful, and definitely lighthearted.

About the Author

Margaret Mears, M.D. is trained in Internal Medicine and has been a physician for over thirty years. While in Medical school, her professors told fellow students that over seventy percent of patients' problems are not physical. However, the time spent on how to address that percentage was abysmal, perhaps three days out of four years. Early on in her career, Dr. Mears took an active interest in the whole patient, their spiritual, mental, emotional and physical makeup. As well, she studied Chinese medicine, for this doctrine addresses our whole makeup extensively and appropriately.

As a practicing physician, Mears' ability to listen and to consider the whole person won her great acclaim among her peers, as well as patients. Naturally, women's issues were at the forefront. Repeatedly, she saw women being diagnosed as "stressed out," being told "you need to see a psychiatrist;" and treated like they were crazy. As her patients shared their stories she realized that she was dealing with exceptionally courageous, determined, lighthearted people. Soon, men dropped their preconceived barriers. "I'm not going to see any woman doctor," and began seeking her counsel. In sharing their wisdom, doctor and patient developed a healthy respect for each other's experiences.

In 1998, Mears read an article that forever changed her life. Her intrigue soared when she read that writing could be used to help youngsters heal. At that moment, she knew this was her next path. Today, as founder of *Write From Your Heart* ™, Mears leads Creative Writing groups in the Phoenix area. The method used is conducive to improving many types of health problems, on multiple levels. She has been published in The Arizona Family Physician's magazine, and in the Journal of Pharmacy Technology. Her topic? C is for Chuckle: The Power of Laughter in the Workplace.

Mears advocates the use of humor to heal broken spirits as well as bones. She actively practices massage as a therapeutic modality, for she knows the power of touch. She has had her own radio show in the Phoenix area, where guest speakers presented fascinating aspects of healing. Mears' extensive range of study over the years makes her the perfect person to author this book. Her willingness to listen to her patients gave them a sense of truly being heard and gifted her with a wealth of inspiring anecdotes from which to draw.

ABC's of Lighthearted Living
...My Rx
Introduction

My life could never be described as boring, for I have been blessed with myriad experiences, all contributing to my growth and all directly related to decisions I have made along the way. Sometimes I could see this clearly, other times I could recognize no relationship at all and was definitely unwilling to admit it. I have learned to honestly explore these "Why in the h… did this happen to me?" occasions and came to this truth: Yes, I did create them. This was a monumental discovery, a freeing one, because I shifted my perception of life's events. Instead of being a victim, I became the creator, the CEO, the waver of the wand.

"Why or how did this happen to me?" metamorphosed into "What did I do to create this mess?" or, delightfully, "How did I cause this fantastic experience to occur?" At long last I saw that it works both ways. Quick to blame myself (or others) for the "bad" things in my life, I didn't give myself credit for the wonder-full happenings.

In my office as an Internal Medicine physician, this axiom of us as creators of our experience was revealed to me many times over, as angels appeared in the form of patients. (With their permission, I've included some of their personal stories, most of the time with names changed.) So, while I was being honed and fine-tuned into the person I was sent here to be, others were giving me the gifts of their insights, their reflections about their health, longevity, happiness, and energy level. The ironic thing is that these folks hadn't all yet realized this truth for themselves, that they had created their exciting life events, but they sure taught me. That's why we're here, I discovered, to assist each other along life's path.

Let me introduce you to two of my teachers/ mentors/ friends who assisted me greatly in my life. They cheer me on to this day and their wise friendship sustains me.

Pat Schneider is a wonderful writer, lyricist, poet, playwright and editor. She has worked with hundreds of low-income women and families, children, regular folks in other occupations, grieving groups, the abused, etc. She has helped me to find my voice as a writer, and inspired me to follow my dream of assisting others to unmask their life and their voice. Both adults and children will find themselves, because of Pat's influence.

I also took a good look at my life, by way of some spiritual, revealing workshops led by Keith Varnum, a dear friend of mine in Phoenix, AZ. These gatherings changed my life completely for the better. Spiritual leaders say when one is ready to learn, the teacher will appear, and I was ready. Keith continues to assist me in my education and growth as a person.

I learned to be light-hearted instead of succumbing to worry, or dwelling on negative events, thoughts, outcomes that carry more energy to them, even though it's unwanted or lower energy. Some people, when they hear serious stuff, say *"Wow! Isn't that terrible? That happened to me once and it was awful!"* They're sucked right in, back to similar terrible times, and often pass the news on to others: "Did you hear...?"

On the other hand, if you have good news to share, it doesn't always elicit the same reaction from others. They may not be able to relate to your good fortune, because they've never let in a like experience. Or they may be so caught up in the dramatic or traumatic movie of their own life that your news of a significant raise, job offer, wonderful new relationship or your dream vacation trip just flies right through their consciousness. Sometimes friends are actually jealous of the good that comes your way, envious of the fact that others can keep a great outlook on life. They appear jaded when you are happy and vibrant. Their response is often a lackadaisical, "Oh, that's nice. Did I tell you what my S.O.B. boss did to me today?"

Another huge influence in my life these past few years has been some amazing courses I have taken at Landmark Education. Some of their precepts and empowering practices are echoed in this book. Ones such as I can be cause in the matter of my own life and make a huge contribution to others. Or, who we are being is way more important and has greater amazing results for our life than what we do. In my personal life, I see that I have spent countless hours doing, doing, doing, when it is much easier and more rewarding to begin with the way I am being about a situation, or about life for that matter. Rich communication and relationships are not only possible but can be way beyond wonderful. I am so grateful for the friends I've made there and the enhanced beauty of my life as a result. I would highly recommend Landmark's courses to anyone.

In spite of others' reactions, or lack thereof, to our good fortunes, we can and must remember we are the authors of our experience. And, we can live a happy, joy-filled, delighted life.

Here, letter-by-letter is my prescription (Rx) for doing so. It is my wish and dream that what you read will first of all, be a switch to turn up the wattage in the light bulb of your life, and that you will enjoy the words and stories shared herein.

Here we go with the ABCs:

A is for Attitude

attitude: **a:** a settled opinion or way of thinking. **b:** behavior reflecting this.

Now, if the dictionary pros had added **c:** *results dependent on this*, I would be ecstatic. When I first moved to Arizona, my medical office was in Phoenix, I lived in Glendale and really didn't know much about Sun City. I saw, on a regular basis, many retired seniors, and some of them would describe how depressed they were with their living situations.

Sun City is a horrible place to live. There is nothing to do. The neighbors never socialize with each other. The streets are bare. They never come out of their houses. Why doesn't someone plan some social activities? I want to walk, but there isn't anyone to walk with.

I, in my ignorance of the place, soon came to fear the prospect of living anywhere near Sun City or its inhabitants, who spent all their time snoozing, from what those particular patients had conveyed to me. I feared this defeated outlook might be catching, even life-threatening. When the invitation came to make a change in my practice location, it was with trepidation that I finally screwed up my courage to relocate to this retirement community.

Once I had moved, I was shocked, for I met a whole new breed of clients who taught me their point of view, and shared rich details of their lifestyle which was entirely opposed to that other one. Their lives were rich indeed, because of their attitude. I have thankfully discovered that a winning attitude shows up in all ages. This part of the chapter describes seniors. Later, I'll share a story about a youngster that will touch and move you, hopefully inspire you too.

I met a wonderful lady, Micki, who was looking after her ailing mother. She took time for herself and cycled forty to fifty miles every other day, with friends she had met when she had joined a biking group. The relief from stress for her was life-saving. Newcomer Sue shared with me that she spent a few days unpacking, then marched up to her neighbors' homes, rang their doorbells, and introduced herself. Then she invited them over for a cup of tea. From these people, she found two who loved to walk. Off they went three days a week, inviting others to join them. Soon there were ten.

Additional patients informed me of the Recreation Centers, the computer group, chorale, hiking, stained glass classes, and of course, lawn bowling. One raucous couple in their seventies, Adele and Sidney, even led day trips to Laughlin, entertaining a bus load of lively fellow- trekkers on the way.

Then there's Bill Butler. Bill was eighty-one years young at the time of this writing. He walked with a walker, wore braces on both legs and had a severe tremor of both hands. His hands shook so badly that he had trouble turning a page. He had to cover his pen with a cylinder of foam so that he could grasp it firmly enough to write. Can you imagine this outer picture of Bill?

Well, now look at the inner aspect of this fascinating person. He had the most amazing attitude, for he walked into our Creative Writing gathering and said, "I'm here. I want to write!" Each week he had us in stitches because of his crazy sense of humor and his spunk. Can you imagine yourself taking a writing class, sitting in front of twelve or so other folks and shaking your way through each week of putting pen to paper? Consider how much earlier he had to get up and be prepared to leave home, just to get to us on time.

The interesting aspect is that after a couple of weeks, we just welcomed Bill and forgot that he had this condition. We had the greatest respect for him. "Oh, if I had let this get me down," he shared one day, "I'd be long gone by now." If there was a chapter in this book titled C is for Courage, Bill would be in that one too.

Forever etched in my heart is the memory of two ladies with horrible Rheumatoid Arthritis. They suffered daily. Yet, they were the happiest, cheeriest, twinkle-in-their-eye people that I had ever met. "How do you do it?" I asked one of them at the time of her office visit. As she slowly struggled from her chair, and put her two gnarled, swollen hands on my arms, she stated, "I never give in to this. Nothing will have the power to destroy my happiness." Wow.

A new truth hit me after several months. Actually I had learned it on an intellectual level, as a platitude, but not on a deep experiential plane. And that was the striking fact that the ones with the upbeat attitudes stayed healthier longer, on all levels: mental, emotional, spiritual and physical. Why, these folks were really *living!* Their lives and their health were a direct reflection of their buoyant attitude. They cared enough about themselves to eat nutritious food, exercise frequently, attend to their spiritual needs and hang out with positive people. Sun City, AZ has a huge volunteer population. They've learned the secret of giving and serving others too.

Dr. Bernie Siegel, in his book, *Love, Medicine and Miracles*, states, "Everyone can be an exceptional patient. The best time to start is before getting sick."

I was very fortunate as a youngster, to have parents and a grandma who would read to me before I drifted off to sleep. I loved to listen to stories. Soon I would memorize all the words so that, by the age of five, I could "read" these tales to Nana or Mom as they sat beside me on the sofa, turning the pages.

One of my most favorite stories was that of the little Engine that could. Remember that one? He'd chug along, then coming to the base of the monumental hill, he'd puff, "I think I can, I think I can." He screwed up his courage, put his all into it and headed up the steep grade with a full head of steam, "I know I can, I know I can." Finally, after reaching the peak, he coasted along and whistled happily, "I knew I could, I knew I could!"

I read and re-read that story so many times. Even into my adulthood, I remembered that spunky engine, his persistence in spite of the heavy load. That attitude got me through medical school, over broken hearts, extensive surgery, and many other life challenges. At mile twenty-four of a marathon, that little engine came to my rescue, and whistled me into the finish line. I am forever grateful to Watty Piper, the author of that childhood tale. It has saved my life as I remember that it is attitude that gets you over the hills of life. And if that attitude is a happy one, so much the better.

Now, meet Desmond, as told to me by his grandma. I took the liberty of putting her words into story form.

Desmond, six years old, grunted as he tied the last loop in his sneakers. "Okay, Mom, I'm going to run!" He grinned.

"Just a minute, son, we might have to turn those shoes around. What do you think?"

Bending way over to survey his feet, Desmond let out a cry. He clapped his hand over his mouth and giggled, "Oh, no, Desmond did it again!" Sitting back down on the lowest step of the stairs by the front door, he untied his shoes and laid them in front of his toes.

"Okay Momma, I got it right this time, didn't I?" His mother nodded up and down, tousling his hair. "You sure did, honey. Come on, how about I put one on for you and you do the other one?"

"No, that won't work; my shoe won't fit on your foot. Your foot is way too big." Then he laughed out loud, "Ha Ha, Mom, I made a joke!"

"Yes, you did. Better run now. Your friends will wonder where you are."

Desmond scooted out to Mrs. Baker's car, waiting by the curb. He and his friends were off to practice running for the Special Limpics, as he called them.

At the track, Desmond practiced hard. His arms stuck out at the sides as he half-walked, half-jogged along the cinder track. The first few weeks, he could make it only to the blue bleachers. He thought that was great fun and even came up with an ingenious plan to measure his progress. He began to count the number of bleacher sections that he could pass, and their color. The first few weeks, he could make it only to the blue ones.

But on the fourth week, he scared the pigeons, sending them spiraling upwards, when he shrieked, "Mrs. Baker, Mrs. Baker, I made it to the yellow seats!"

Finally, the day of the big race arrived. As the first sun's rays crept over Desmond's bedspread, he sat straight up in bed. He ran hollering into his parents' room, "Today's the race. Mom. Dad. Get up. We got to go!"

His father sat up sleepily, wiping his eyes. "Whoa, slow down, Des. It doesn't start for four hours. Come on, climb up here beside me." Desmond crawled up beside his dad, his feet swinging over the side of the bed. "Des, I want you to know how proud I am of you. No matter what happens today, we love you." Desmond grinned back and reassured his father, "I'm going to win today, Dad. Aren't I, Momma?"

"Well, we sure hope so, but just in case…"

Shaking his head, Desmond repeated, "I'm going to win. I am." Desmond's mom and dad smiled, and then slowly got out of bed. "Okay, you need to have a shower now, and then some breakfast."

"Ah, Mom! We'll miss the track meet," Desmond cried in his most convincing tone of voice. It was no use. Into the shower he went. Desmond washed himself all over faster then he ever had before, dried off with his favorite blue towel, and shimmied into his official race-day shorts.

He ran downstairs and jumped into his seat at the family table. His dad looked up from the morning paper, his mouth a big 'O'. "Are you ready so soon?" he asked. Then looking long and hard at his watch, he sputtered, "Let's see. Two more hours!"

"I am eating my toast now, Dad. See? You promised we'd go as soon as I finish my breakfast!"

With a twinkle in his eye, his dad chuckled, "Yes, son, I did promise. Let's go, Mom, so Des can win that race."

And win he did. Desmond walked and loped and ran past the blue seats, hurried past the yellow section, scurried around the green ones, and finally came to a stop next to a flag waving cheerily at the finish line.

Desmond bowed when they presented him with the blue ribbon, and blew kisses at the people in the stands, clapping like crazy.

He won another award that day too. Just as the master of ceremonies handed him another ribbon, this one with a big 'A' on it, Desmond hollered, "Yes, sir. A is for Attitude. I did it!"

B is for Balance

Remember the teeter-totter from your childhood days? When you were in balance with a friend on the other end, you could sail up and down with joyful abandon and very little effort. A little push with your toes and off you flew into the air; then a push by your buddy and down you gently came to the ground. There was an unspoken agreement between the two of you that you'd keep each other going. There was cooperation, synchronicity, trust and fun. What happened if your friend on the other end decided he had to leave, or the imp in him decided to jump off? Suddenly, you hit bottom and *your* bottom with a whack. The only difference between that experience and the one when your adult life is out of balance is this: When you and I were children, we learned to recognize the warning signs, before we became off-kilter. We knew the feelings we were experiencing meant something. We had learned to recognize that the nervousness and fluttery stomach meant we were going to hit bottom. We were out of balance and knew it.

What we can do as adults is to relearn to recognize the signs of becoming unbalanced, so we can do something about our situation before it affects the very fabric of our lives. We would be wise to recognize when we're becoming heavy, and how to remain light (and lighthearted) even in the face of heaps of adversity on the other end of our teeter-totter. When our friend (spouse, buddy, lover) leaps off the other end, we know we're in danger of plummeting precipitously to ground zero and can be prepared. It all comes down to maintaining our balance.

I see us as whole beings, not just physical ones. We need to balance the four parts of our SELF:

Physical,
Mental,
Spiritual,
Emotional.

Each aspect of us and the time we devote to it has to balance the other parts. It doesn't work to overdo our physical exercise and totally neglect our emotional well being, for example.

One client, W.W., decided he'd feel better if he quit smoking and worked out. He took out a membership at the community gym and signed up with a personal trainer. By the time a year was up, he had lost thirty pounds and ten percent of his body fat. He was hooked and soon was spending one and one half hours in the morning working out with weights as well as extensive cardiovascular exercises. A couple of days a week he stopped by the gym "just for an hour" of weight-lifting in the evening. Soon, he noticed he hadn't talked to his girlfriend all week. Worse, she hadn't called him to complain! He began to have to take a mid-day nap, as he was so tired. He became frustrated with lack of response to his weight-lifting goals.

As you can see, what started out as a good idea for self-improvement, turned into a control monster. His emotional life (relationships) suffered; his mental state was one of frustration; and his spiritual life, what was that? He had stopped meditating. He had no time. And his minister hadn't seen him for months.

Another friend was Wendy. Wendy was pretty fit already. She walked six days a week but she was bored, didn't feel like going out with friends, and her sleep began to suffer. Let's face it, she was depressed.

Wendy had heard that it did you good to volunteer to help others. Sitting at her kitchen table one morning, she reflected on the behavior of the children in her family when she was around. Her nieces and nephews flocked to her, pulling her sleeves and grabbing her hand.

"Aunt Wendy! Wanna see my science project?"

"Aunt Wendy. Come look at my new puppy!"

"Auntie, will you read with me?" said quiet Amy, as she crawled into Wendy's lap.

When she realized she'd always had a gift for children, Wendy called the crisis nursery and trained to be a volunteer. Her whole life changed as a result. She now knew she was of value in this world. This fed her spiritual self, which in turn lifted her emotions from depression to joy and she began to feel whole once more. Where she had been flailing around emotionally and failing in her relationship with her boyfriend, she approached him with a new zest for life, creating fantastic talks and fun outings.

Mentally, her creativity kicked into play. She developed several new games for the children at the crisis nursery, increasing their light-heartedness as well as hers.

She looked around at her little charges one day as they played, running in circles and giggled with them. She felt light and in balance.

Anyone who is a physician, is married to one or tries to reach one and can't, knows firsthand what is meant by a life out of balance. It is not only physicians who fall into this group; it is simply that I am most familiar with them. Anyone with a hectic job can relate. We need balance between work and home, between the demands of patients, clients, assignments, case load, deadlines, and that of our most precious relationships. If we are to have a lighthearted, balanced life, we must begin to make choices that will keep us in balance. Most times, it takes a concerted, committed effort to do so, but it is entirely worth it. Our marriage and other love relationships will blossom, our children will miraculously change; our stress levels diminish noticeably. We will awaken refreshed and alive.

The business person reading this may think their business will suffer. Absolutely not. It will grow exponentially as you acquire a new understanding of purpose, people, their relative importance in your world, and you in theirs.

If you have doubts, do yourself a favor for thirty days. Remember balance in all things and watch for astounding changes in many aspects of your life.

C is for Creativity

How often have you heard someone say, "Oh, Susan is so creative. She paints amazing landscapes."

Or, "George can whip together metal creations out of nothing! I'm not creative at all. Wish I was."

That was Judy's song. She shied away from doing crafts. "I can't do that," she'd shrug. She repeated the "I can't do it, I'm not creative," refrain for so long that she believed it. Her hubby, Joel, didn't feel he was creative either, so they were a matched set. They had been patients for about four years, wonderfully warm people, and both about one hundred pounds overweight. Bored to tears, they'd sit each night for hours, nibbling their desires away.

However, one day, Joel watched Home Gardening on the Do It Yourself channel and took off to Home Depot after the third episode. He cajoled Judy into helping him clear a section in their back yard that had lain bare, brown and choked with weeds for the past seven years. Something clicked in Judy's brain now too. It was only a little urging, a distant memory of happy times in another garden, but she listened to the prompting and it propelled her forward. Together, the pair worked for hours, and created a lovely garden, complete with Japanese lanterns, stonework and a path to meander along.

Sitting in the midst of their creation one Sunday afternoon, Judy looked towards the back wall of their home. She jumped up and told Joel, "Let's clear this area under the windows. I want flower boxes. I want to be able to look out my kitchen window and see bright, happy flowers."

At first, Joel was dubious about her suggestion, but not wanting to deter her new-found enthusiasm, he agreed. "Sure, that would be great. Tomorrow after work, let's go check them out."

Rob Daugherty, in his article, "*Understanding the Mind: 5 Keys to Creativity,*" tells us that we all have a network of cells in our brains where every experience we've ever had is stored. These experiences are able to be called upon at any time and can serve to inspire us.

In Judy's case, working outside in the dirt had triggered a happy memory from her past, digging side by side years ago with her favorite grandpa. He had a knack for creating masterpieces in his garden, turning each home into a vista of color, places for family and neighbors to indulge in an "awe-some" moment. In their model home park, he won awards every year for his abilities, and Judy remembered all that when she was down on her hands and knees, weeding and planting beside Joel.

Deepak Chopra spoke at a conference one sunny spring day in La Jolla, Ca. There he narrated a most amazing story that illustrates this point so clearly, the power of our minds to access those stored memories and from there, create.

Riding his exercise bicycle very early one morning, Dr. Chopra suddenly remembered a diabetic patient of his, whom he had not seen, nor spoken to for over twenty years, Mr. Samuel Richmond. (Name has been changed.) He recalled him that day, as clearly as if the man were there beside him. In his private practice years before as an endocrinologist, Dr. Chopra phoned Mr. Richmond daily, as his blood sugars would vacillate wildly. "This is Dr. Chopra, how are you today, and what are your blood sugar readings?"

He then would give him instructions as to the insulin dosage for that day. As you can imagine, the two men grew quite close.

"I wonder if I can recall his phone number," he thought, as he pedaled along. Right then, he couldn't, but he reassured himself, "It will come, and when it does, I will call that man."

Later that evening, while eating dinner with his family, he suddenly jumped up from the table, grabbed pen and paper from the sideboard, and wrote down a telephone number. He walked to the phone with a grin on his face, and dialed the number.

When a male voice answered, he asked, "Is this Mr. Samuel Richmond?"

"Why, yes it is," the man said.

"This is Dr. Chopra. How are you and how is your blood sugar today?"

As you can imagine, the patient was astounded, as well as ecstatic to hear Dr. Chopra's voice, and the two friends had a wonderful reunion on the phone.

But he uses this story to illustrate not the power of our memory for its own sake, but to remind us that we too can summon up the talents, cherished activities and forgotten dreams we allowed time for, years ago, before we had to be "responsible."

Inventions, fascinating ideas, things that thrilled us, now lie inside us, waiting to be rediscovered. This is creativity. It resides in every single one of us, omitting no-one.

I am blessed, by living in Arizona, to have many patients and friends who are Native Americans. Several of them shared with me their customs as parents, watching their little ones. They make a habit of observing their youngsters at play, and then take note of what the children do for "fun." Children are very inventive, imaginative and can have a great playtime with very simple items. But the elders soon learned that what their young ones do for play, what they are naturally drawn to, is what fascinates them the most. And so, as the child grows, they encourage them to pursue those things as vocations or avocations, for then they will be truly happy.

Okay, you might smirk, so I'm creative. How in the heck do I find my skill, or something I'd love to do?

Here are a couple of hints:

1. An easy exercise to do is to sit down and write a list of what really fascinated or intrigued you as a child. Don't pass judgment upon yourself for your creative idea. Each of us has the ability to create in a way that would mystify others.
2. Get out the phone book; go to the public library or community center and sign up for classes in an area that enthralls you. Many craft stores hold fun workshops which are very reasonably priced. They vary from cake decorating to quilting, framing to candle-making. Hardware supply stores such as Lowe's and Home Depot put on very informative classes

every week, where you can learn to set tile, refurbish your bathroom, build that flower box. Plant nurseries have consultants on staff, just waiting to share their skills, who will be thrilled that you are so interested. Most often these establishments charge only nominal fees, because you will purchase your necessary supplies there.

3. Talk to someone who is happily creating in an area that fascinates you. See how they got started. Ask questions. Perhaps you could very quietly watch them a couple of times. (I say quietly because many creative folks do not want a noisy interrupter standing at their side chattering away. Respect that.)

So your neighbor can rebuild a car engine? Don't feel bad. I bet he can't grow vegetables like you do, or whip up a delicious dinner to feed the neighborhood. Does your friend sing songs that take your breath away and you can't hold a tune? Bet they can't tell a story to a group of children, kneeling rapt at attention at the library, like you can. So the guy down the street can paint beauty onto a canvas and your attempts look like those of a two-year-old with finger paints? Bet he can't write word pictures that can make a reader weep or laugh hysterically.

Do your thing, and do it with zest. Dip into your well and enjoy every moment of your creative gift. It's all inside you, waiting to be set free.

D is for Dare To Dream

You got to have a dream
If you don't have a dream
How you gonna have a dream come true?
Happy Talk, **Oscar Hammerstein II**

I want to tell you a story.

Once there was a tall, tall tree, way up in the tall, tall mountains. A pine tree, I think it was. Mr. and Mrs. Swallow met, married, and decided to raise a family. Mr. Swallow flew around the mountaintop, collecting soft undergrowth, moss, pieces of string, and boughs. Mrs. Swallow decorated their nest and promptly rearranged the items he brought home each day.

One bright spring morning, Mrs. Swallow awoke, stretched her wings and knew it was time. She could feel little feet pushing to get out, arms flailing against the sides of her abdomen. Even a tiny peep? She sat in the nest and pushed and pushed. Mr. Swallow flapped his wings and cheeped loudly, "Yes! You can do it, dear. Come on! I want to see our little Sammy or Sally." He strode about from branch to branch, chest feathers puffed out. Lo and behold, Mrs. Swallow gave one big push and out popped a little girl. Then, to her shocked surprise, another one right behind. (I know, I know, swallows have eggs. I am using my poetic license to play a little with this story.)

Mr. and Mrs. Swallow were so excited, they flapped their wings and jumped up and down. Mr. Swallow flew off to their friends' nests, banging on their doors, and chirping, Guess what? Guess what?

Sally and Sadie grew up. Sally was the perfect little bird. She helped her mother with the cleaning, went dutifully to school, did her home (nest) work every evening. Even when the light filtering through the trees made it hard to read, she labored away on her Home Ec, crafts, wildlife and bird watching classes. Sally never smoked and never swore. She sang sweet songs in the

Pinesville church choir.

Sadie, on the other hand, was a bit of a rascal. She had things to do and places to be. When her father asked her to help sweep, or wash dishes, or take out the garbage, she'd say, "Just a minute, Pops." Then she'd hop about on the branches, pluck stray grubs from their homes and sing rock with the Cardinals next door. They were cool dudes.

Mr. and Mrs. Swallow would just shake their heads, "Sadie, what will we do with you?"

Finally, she'd give in and help with chores.

But Sadie had a dream. She wanted to see the world. "Surely there's more to do than hang around dull old Pinesville," she'd say. "I'm going to travel," she'd confide to Sally some nights, when they lay in their little bunk beds whispering after lights out.

"I'm going to fly to the Mississippi, sail down the river. I will have my own band and be famous. I want to make a difference in this world somehow."

Sally would laugh at her, "Sadie Swallow, who do you think you are? You can't take chances like that. You're small, the world is big, and one of your wings is bent. Besides, you need to stay in college and get a degree. Stay here where you'll be safe."

"No!" Sadie said.

So one day she scrunched up her eyes and her courage, placed her little toes on the edge of the nest and took off. She spread her wings, did somersaults in the sky, whooped and hollered. "Yahoo!"

Oh, Sadie had hard times to be sure. One night, she was shocked when her supposed friend said, "No, you can't sleep at my nest tonight." So, she slept in the park, hunkered down beneath an old codger on the park bench. The guy snored real loud, but protected her from the rain, and what the heck, even fed her crumbs the next morning.

Sadie flew and swooped and dived and sang. Sometimes, she missed her family dearly, and would scrape together enough funds to send home a warble gram. But she wouldn't trade her life for anything.

Finally, she teamed up with a handsome tenor she met on the road, Roberto Robin. Together they formed their own band, The Rockin' Robins, and toured the country. Eventually, they set up a scholarship fund for birds who showed promise. Mr. and Mrs. Swallow were so proud of Sadie. Even sister Sally whistled loudly in applause at her first musical concert.

Sadie was ecstatic, living the life she'd dreamed of forever. It all began with that first brave step out of the nest.

Melanie, in her early forties, bounced into my office one day for a trucker's physical exam. Pretty, bright, fit and full of energy, she hopped up onto the exam table with ease.

"Whatever made you choose to become a truck driver?" I asked her. Truthfully, I was incredulous. She certainly didn't look like many of the other female candidates who had plopped down on that exam table in previous weeks. Nor did she fit my pictures of a woman who could handle 80,000 pound rigs.

She sat back and answered with a grin, "I've always had a dream of driving these trucks. When we were kids, my truck-driver dad would take us along in the summer, and I fell in love with the road, the people we met, the adventure of it all. I guess I wanted to explore parts of myself that I've never experienced before; find out what I'm really made of."

I was impressed for I had learned of the many ardors of the business. As I examined her, and tested her strength and flexibility, I wasn't surprised to find that all was perfect. Her physical strength was echoed by the flexibility of her attitude. Here was a person who had dared to live her dream.

Whether Melanie trucks across America three times or three hundred, she will be happy. Those who come in contact with her will find themselves smiling a little brighter. When we follow our dream, it opens the space for others around us to do so as well. Follow your dream and Happy Trucking!

E: Enjoy Each Day as If it were Your Last

When I was twenty-six, I received a frantic call from my mother. "Mom, what's wrong?" She then told me that the wife of their building manager had dropped dead, just like that. No warnings, no illness preceding it. Suddenly, she was gone, at the age of fifty-two. Her husband was stunned, deeply upset. "Oh, we had so many things planned for when we retire, trips to take. She wanted so badly to see a play last week. I told her, No, we must wait to spend our money," he sobbed. "I wish I had given her all that."

I still remember my mother's parting wise advice on the phone, "You must live as if each day were your last, dear." Those words made a huge impact on me, changing my life, my priorities and how I choose to spend my time. Obviously, over the years, there have been a few times when my life as a physician was all too serious. But someone would pop up and remind me of those sage words. Actually, now I would expand that wise maxim to "Live as if each *moment* of every day…"

One of my lovely patients, Sally H., epitomized the opposite of this point of view. Her husband was very supportive, but even he was about to give up. No matter how he tried to help her, Sally always found something about which to worry or be depressed. She could have won a blue ribbon for perfecting the art of fretting. In fact, I am sure she had several such awards at home, that she kept hidden in a shoebox in her closet. Several times a day, she'd take them down from the shelf, count them, sort them and relive each episode. She'd castigate herself for her supposed role in each event, and then add a few more from yesterday, to worry about tomorrow. And if it weren't something wrong with her, she'd worry about her children, the neighbor, the pharmacist's wife, and the dog. Sound familiar? Lighthearted, she was not.

Sally came to see me with high blood pressure, skin rashes and diarrhea. Somehow, that did not surprise us. She had no energy and would take to her bed for hours at a time, feeling exhausted. It was hard for her to enjoy any part of her day. Suggestions from well-meaning family, friends, or me were always met with these two words first: "Yes, but…"

After a full workup revealed no serious physical cause for her maladies, and after counseling Sally over the course of many office visit hours, she finally admitted she was a worrywart "magna cum laude." She'd graduated at the top of her class in this subject, she admitted one day, with her first small grin. She realized what a toll was being exacted on her body and her relationships, and decided she'd rather embark on her ME degree: Master of Enjoyment.

Here was her new schedule:

Every morning she took her little make-believe box off the shelf, withdrew a piece of paper on which she'd written all the people, places and things she fretted about and set the kitchen timer. Then she stewed over them, worried, frowned, and wrung her hands in despair for ten minutes. When the timer ding-dinged, she stopped, then put the box back in its place, on that high shelf in her closet. Ten minutes was all she allowed herself each day engaged in this useless pursuit. Then she made a conscious choice to spend the rest of the day looking for, actually stalking, that which made her happy.

Sally went to her favorite coffee shop the first day of her new adventure, and sat down with pen and paper. She wrote:

"If I had all the time, money and energy I needed, and nobody was stopping me, I would…"
then,
"What I have always yearned to do and never did, is…"

At first the answers came slowly, but pretty soon, to her amazement, the words began to pour out and the page filled up. Filled with her dreams, her desires that she'd never realized or admitted, even to herself. She left the restaurant exhilarated and rushed home to share this with her husband, who was amazed at the transformation of his wife. They sat after dinner that evening and poured over her list. Pretty soon, he was making out his list, as the realization hit home for him, that he had given up a lot of his dreams, in his concern for her. Together, they planned some trips and excursions and actually took them.

Three weeks later, my nurse came into my office, message pad in hand. Sally H. wants to see you. "Oh no," I moaned. "I thought she was doing so well. What can be wrong now? Get her in here at three," I told Steph.

Three o'clock came and sure enough, there sat Sally. I stood for a moment outside the door and prayed for strength and wisdom, to know what to do next. Then, slowly turning the door handle, I entered the room. There to my amazed eyes sat a new person! Gone was her rash, which had plagued her for years; her diarrhea had disappeared, and she was smiling. Her blood pressure was remarkable, the best it had ever been. In fact, we began the happy process of decreasing her meds.

Sally is a different person today, thankfully. She and her husband plan adventures together, sometimes just a night out at a different restaurant, other times a day trip. She has time and energy for her friends. She has learned how to enjoy each day and realizes that if she hadn't, the day that was her last would have come all too soon.

If any of this true tale strikes home to you, take out that notepad, and make out your list, then go do it. Enjoy each day as if it were your last.

F is for Furniture

Keith was a tall, buff fifteen-year-old, captain of his football team, son of an attorney dad and a courtroom reporter mom, well inured in the rules of the game of life as well as sports. Keith was a rebel of sorts. Raised so strictly, he had to test out his parents' teachings for himself. He was also a very spiritual person, even at that young age. He had dreams of angels, bringing him supportive messages. Spiritual mentors would appear to him on the lake as he and a buddy were fishing; in his room while studying. Keith was smart. He told no one. In the sixties, you didn't breathe a word about such happenings.

Keith's rebellious nature acted up at times; normal for a high-school kid but more so when the establishment and its pronouncements suffocated him and his friends.

One such afternoon when the suppression seemed just too much, he sneaked out to the back wall of the school. With a paintbrush he began to scrawl his frustration onto the rough concrete wall. He had completed the F and was on the down stroke of the U, when, out of the corner of his eye, he saw two men approaching him. He heard at the same time, the deep, resonant voice of the high-school principal. Brush in mid-air, his arm still held high, Keith halted. Panicked, he thought to himself, *Oh no! What other word begins with F –U - ? Quick! Quick!* He snapped his mental fingers. All of a sudden the word flashed across his mind, the word that would save his hide. He shuffled his feet, bounced up and down on his toes and heaved a sigh of relief.

Completing the downward portion of the U, he continued. R –N – I – T –U –R- E. The two adults standing behind him on the pavement spoke not a word. About the time he reached the T, he heard a distinctive Harrumph! and clearing of throats.

"Young man, what do you think you are doing?" they hollered as they walked towards him. Keith, in pretended surprise, jumped and turned around to face them. His explanations weren't the best. He was punished with hours of study hall, but not nearly so severely as if he'd used the other "F- word."

When Keith related this story to a group of us adults over lunch, we howled with laughter. I had to catch my breath before I could ask him, "Didn't you think of the word FUN? It is much shorter than Furniture!" He smiled, "Yes, that's true. But I couldn't come up with it that fast, and besides, life wasn't all that much fun in those days. Now, it is a very different story."

"What do you feel made the difference?" we asked. "What did you do?"

"There were several things," he explained, sliding back his chair. "I started to hang out with fun people, and began to do what I loved: classes in paint, photography. I studied movie-making, which totally enthralled me. Besides the subject matter being so fascinating, I saw so many different aspects and sides to people. There was another world out there, so different from my own hometown.

"I stopped following other folks' rules if they didn't fit with who I really was," he went on. By this point we were all leaning forward, arms on the table, wondering what he'd say next.

"I made and followed my own maxims, ones that suited me. Every morning, when I woke up, I lay there in my bed and pretended that I felt how I really wanted to feel---happy, joyous, fulfilled, acknowledged. Every day I did this, for months. Finally, one afternoon, I suddenly realized that I had been happy all day, upbeat, satisfied, complete. I hadn't had to pretend."

Our conversation was enlightening, as well as hilarious, and true. As I maneuvered my car through traffic on the way home, I reflected on Keith's words. I thought about F is for FURNITURE, F is for FUN, instead of all the other connotations some people place on that letter: Failure, Fat, Fool, Foreigner, Frivolous, Foreboding, and Foreclosure, to name just a few.

After that I decided to fill my life with fun every day, even if it was only for fifteen minutes. My life changed too.

Try it; whatever brings a laugh from your heart. Jogging? Playing with your kids or grandkids? Flopping down in a Fluffy overstuffed chair in front of a fire? Listening to music? Walking in the woods? Jumping up and down at a sports event. When was the last time you really let loose? Try it for a week, then another. Life will be richer and so will you.

F is for Furniture:

My wish for you is that you can create a space to kick back, read to your heart's content or Fill the room with Fantastic music; pull out the faded piano bench that's grown forlorn in the corner, flip open the lid and play a Frivolous tune; Frequent a Farmer's market and rustle up a feast; have a picnic with your special someone, in the comfort of your own bed. Find a Forgotten Friend and refresh your connection! Give a massage (and get one). Get in touch with the spirit of you, in your favorite pew that's been vacant. Spend time alone, nurturing that part of you that has had to be responsible for God knows how many years. Sometimes it is a joy simply to sit and do nothing. When did we last give ourselves guilt-free permission to do that?

Fill your life with Fantastic Furniture, accept your own Foibles, have Fun each day!

G is for Gratitude

I don't know who first suggested it, or I would give them credit here. But some wise soul suggests we make a gratitude list every evening before we go to sleep. Just a few minutes of our time daily with pen and paper, to jot down a few events or people for which we are thankful, can bring great rewards in many aspects of our lives. One fun aspect of this habit is that as we become more attentive to those acts for which we are grateful and know we are to write them down, we tend to be on the lookout for them to occur. It makes the whole day go more smoothly because we begin to see life through different eyes.

Not only that, once we recognize that such behavior can make a huge difference for us, we can begin to play with the idea of passing acts of kindness on to others.

We sleep better, surely. We can see possibilities in situations that appeared to be hopeless; create viable solutions; experience more energy to handle ongoing stress; increase our faith and re-affirm our Source of help; we develop a history, of knowing that every situation will turn out for the best, even when it certainly appears to be the opposite. Some of you can think of other benefits of the gratitude attitude. Jot them down now.

"Yeah, sure, easy for you to say," you scoff. "You didn't just lose your best friend. What's to be grateful about that?" (How about all the wonderful times you shared? What you learned about love? What you came to know about your lovability?)

"Well, I just lost my job. I find it very difficult to see benefits in that right now!"

Yes, there are times when it is difficult to recognize the positive in a terrible condition, happening, breakup, etc. But over the years, I have found that there is always, *ALWAYS* in italics and capitals, something to be thankful for. It may be one tiny item, one miniscule unimportant detail to be grateful for, but at least it's one. The next day, we may see another. It gets us through the tough times in life. It doesn't erase all negative feelings from the moment, but does make it easier to feel those feelings and move on.

"Another door will always open, dear," I can still hear my eighty year old patient, Ernie, tell me years ago. I have learned to adopt that posture, feel the pain of the door that slammed in my face, and walk through the new opening.

Sometimes, it may take months for us to see the benefit of a relationship ending, an illness that took forever to resolve. But if we can develop the gratitude attitude and incorporate it as part of whom we are, we can learn to see inner meanings of events sooner. And, when we get really good at it, we can discover reasons to be grateful even as they are happening.

"Ah, ha!" we shout as we see with clarity the deeper meaning of it all. We catch ourselves being grateful for having sick day benefits at our job. And the reality may strike home as we lie in our bed with diarrhea, vomiting, or a wracking cough, for example, that what we really needed was a quiet day to ourselves. Time to lie around and do nothing, or read that great book we always put off, out of guilt, because we 'should' be doing this or that. We can then choose in our wisdom simply to take a day off next time, not becoming ill in order to have what we know we need.

If we had railed against our illness and gone into our Why me? whine instead of gratitude, we may never have seen the greater purpose, may have stayed ill longer and definitely not made the link to positive change for our future.

Helen Keller, who was both deaf and blind, said, "All my life I have tried to avoid… losing my childhood sense of wonderment. It is as natural for me to believe that the richest harvest of happiness comes with age, as it is to believe that true sight and hearing are within, not without." Another of Miss Keller's truisms: "Keep your face to the sunshine and you cannot see the shadow."

To whom can we be grateful?
1. God, or our spiritual head of our belief.
2. Our family.
3. Our friends.
4. Ourselves. Don't forget to praise yourself and be thankful for your own growth as a person.

Behind every event for which we are thankful, there are a series of other events, created by people. So a person leaving their job at TJ Maxx, for example, manifests an opening for you. Someone you don't even know is cooperating in your unfolding of miracles and opportunities. It happens every day.

Several weeks ago, my youngest son, Kelly, called me to ask my advice. He had made a deposit on a house he was to rent and had been ecstatic as the day drew near. The excitement in his voice was obvious as he described the huge fenced backyard for his boys to play in, the perfect rent amount; the reliable roommate; many things for which he was grateful. "This weekend, Mom," he had cheered a few days earlier.

Now he was on the line again. The landlord had called him to apologize, as he had sold the house and now my son was unable to move in. I could hear the disappointment in his voice and I immediately went into my dissertation about the illegality of what the landlord had done. But then Kelly interrupted me, and said, "Mom, I just wanted to ask you what benefits you could see in this happening to me, because I am really having a hard time feeling anything besides angry."

I was stunned and shifted gears in a flash. He didn't need any of my well-meant advice. He yearned to continue to know magic, to feel appreciation for life's vicissitudes.

Together, we were able to come up with at least two reasons to be grateful in this situation. One was that he now wouldn't have to move twice, a huge savings of emotional and physical energy, time and funds. The other is that he could find a home even more perfect than this one, which actually was turning out to require a lot of "fixing up."

I was proud of my son. We finished our conversation with both of us feeling much lighter about the whole situation. Sometimes, when our dreams are dashed, an alternate 'dream-come-true' can appear.

Remember the Gratitude Attitude. As we live each day this way, it will bring much light and lightheartedness into our lives and the lives of others, as we share it.

H is for Higher Self

Higher self. Inner being. Intuition. Spirit. How can developing or recognizing this part of us keep us more lighthearted?

First of all, it will save us from many a decision or choice that is wrong for us. Instead of reaping sorrow, rejection or decline in our joy, we will garner happiness, peace, and contentment, if we learn to depend on our inner voice.

For the newcomer, it is much fun to notice and then record the times our intuition is right on. Make it a game. Learn from these occasions and you will find they occur more often. Or at least they seem to. In reality, it is because we actually recognize those inner promptings more accurately.

Knowing that your higher self wants better for you than you have ever dreamed, is a great stress-reducer. Wouldn't it be wonderful, relaxing and energizing to know that you do not have to worry constantly about paying for the mortgage, energy bills, clothing for your children, or that very necessary new car?

To be assured that this money will flow to you, while you are going about your day is definitely load-lightening! You may be hard at work as usual, but very happy while you're at it.

Our ego wants safety, is threatened by change, wants only to fulfill itself and keep us right where we are. Our Higher self, however, wants the best for us, enjoys risks and change, (which isn't really "risky" because Higher self knows the answers already and won't get you in over your head); thrives on the adventure of our growth.

Higher self is available to guide us in many areas of our lives, not just financial. If you glean wisdom from your Higher self, you'll possess certainty in the area of relationship. You won't have to worry or stress if Mr. Supposedly Wonderful or Ms. Suddenly Summer is the right one for you. In a very short while, you'll know. You can leave the sleepless nights, tossing covers off, and nail-biting to someone else.

Helen S. was a lovely, forty-something, adventurous, crazy-sense-of-humor person. She took good care of herself, exercised at the gym, and had a positive attitude. However, she lacked confidence in her capability to survive after retirement. She felt like she'd never have enough financially to live a wonderful life.

So Helen would jump into any relationship with a man who was rich, or seemed to be. One after the other, she dated men who would meet her needs of survival, but she never stopped to look at other factors, like kindliness, caring, cleanliness, self-respect and respect for others. She never asked her Higher self, her inner knowing, if this or that man was really right for her. If he had funds, she'd simply fit herself into his mold and pray.

One day though, Helen woke up. A light inside grew from a glimmer to a beacon, as she realized her self-worth and began to listen to that inner wisdom. She finally learned to ask, Is this person right for me? Do they fulfill a lot of my needs? Previously she'd spent every relationship working hard to prove that she filled his needs, and struggling to show she was good enough. In the end, she was exhausted, exasperated and his ex.

Now Helen takes an honest look at her love life and moves on when she knows intuitively that it's not right. No more worry. Much more energy, enthusiasm for life, great friends, new interests. She dresses to please herself, travels, has learned to run a computer, something she thought she'd never do, and is fun to be with. Recently, she met a wonderful man at a seminar she attended. Helen definitely walks lighthearted throughout her day.

It is best to research some situations, but we can also use our intuition in many aspects of our life. How does that new home you saw yesterday with the realtor feel to you? How does it feel in your gut? What was your sense of it this morning? What about that move to a new city you've been contemplating? Ask for guidance. You'll get answers. The business deal you put together yesterday---does it brighten your day today?

Living in full view of Higher self makes us more forgiving. More accepting and compassionate, we are able to see the full picture in situations, the real meaning behind events. We are able to predict outcomes if we follow a certain path.

Following our inner wisdom lightens many paths on our street map of life. Being lighthearted and worry-free rubs off on those around you too. We attract "lightminded" people to us. We bring people like nurse Janie into our circle. She is surrounded by fun, positive, lively friends. She is serene in the midst of personal crisis. If you talk to her, Janie will reflect an attitude of trust, of knowing that her life calamities will right themselves, that answers will come from amazing, unexpected sources. Janie's in touch with her Higher self, in tiny ways as well as in life's challenges, trusting in and following her intuition.

Dr. Wayne Dyer in his great book, *The Power of Intention*, says that whenever he feels downhearted, separate, distanced, he realizes he has separated himself from Source, and gets back there, quickly. Then his life is smooth, at least his place in it is, and I see from what he shared, that he is lighthearted once again.

Kelly was a twenty-two year old father of two boys, aged five and three. He was learning about listening to his inner wisdom. His older son, DaVon, was fascinated with mail. Even at the age of five, he was an avid reader, so his grandparents took turns sending him postcards, greeting cards and simple letters. For some reason, DaVon had it fixed in his mind that the daily newspaper was his mail.

On one torch-hot June morning in Phoenix, while Kelly fixed breakfast, DaVon ran outside to get his "mail" and Darrien to play with his truck.

Kelly was busy flipping pancakes and turning over the sizzling bacon, when he heard a voice inside him say, "Go outside now." He wasn't yet accustomed to heeding such messages, putting it down to fatigue or an overactive imagination, so he shrugged it off and continued cooking. He poured another pancake into the cast iron pan and took a slurp of his orange juice.

The voice came again. "Go outside now."

"Hey, will you check on the boys?" he asked his roommate.

"Oh, they're fine," he responded, "I was just out there."

"Hey, great. Thanks!" Kelly turned off the burner, took the bacon out of the pan and covered it with a plate. As he bent down to open the oven door, he heard the voice, shrieking this time. "***Get your butt outside, before you regret it***."

Finally he listened and ran out the door. He spied Darrien immediately, playing in the sand with his truck. "Darrien, where's your brother?"

"I don't know."

Kelly took off running up his street, down the next, with no success. Returning from his neighbors, he could feel the heat burning the soles of his feet. Sweat poured off him, his heart pounded. Just then, two joggers approached him.

"Is that red Mitsubishi yours?" they asked, pointing.

"Yes, why?"

"You'd better check the trunk. We know it sounds silly, but we heard a voice in there. Are you missing someone?"

Bending over, Kelly heard a faint voice, "Dad, Dad!"

"Oh my God, yes." Kelly grabbed the keys and opened the trunk of his car. There he found DaVon, red-faced, tears streaming, holding out his arms. The Sunday paper was clutched tightly in one of them.

"Son, what were you doing in there?" Kelly cried.

"I was reading my mail in my secret hiding place, and the lid shut," DaVon sobbed. Kelly held him close and rubbed his back. "Come on, let's get you cooled off." He turned to thank the couple, but they were gone.

He was mighty glad he had finally listened to that voice of his Higher self. He wonders what would have happened if he had not heeded it. He has also learned to listen the first time, finding that this voice is reliable, strong and true. He is much happier doing so, his days and his life lighthearted, more productive in many ways.

Like Kelly and Helen S., we too can develop our listening ability, and gain trust in our selves. We all have this capability, this Source from whom can come amazing assistance. Some of us call it our guardian angel. Get to know yours!

I is for Imagine

There are books in which the footnotes,
or the comments scrawled by some reader's hand in the margin
are more interesting than the text. The world is one of these books.
George Santayana (1863-1952)

Just imagine! What a reaction these words arouse in us. I don't know about you, but I go back to the excitement I had as a child and I am ready to hear what comes next.

Visualize, dream, conceive, believe. Sounds like Disney, does it not? Walt Disney knew about the power of the imagination. In fact, his employees/creators were rewarded for tapping into their world of "Just Imagine." Where would we have been as children if we had not been able to travel to Dreamland, Tomorrow Land or Fantasy Land? Where would Walt Disney have been if he had not imagined Mickey Mouse?

In Disney's own words, we hear of Mickey's role:

"Mickey Mouse is to me a symbol of independence. He popped out of my mind onto a drawing pad on a train ride from Manhattan to Hollywood, at a time when business fortunes of my brother Roy and myself were at lowest ebb and disaster seemed right around the corner.

"Born of necessity, the little fellow literally freed us of immediate worry. We are rather indebted to Charlie Chaplin for the idea. We wanted something appealing and we thought of a tiny bit of a mouse that would have some of the wistfulness of Chaplin, a little fellow trying to do the best he could."

Roy and Walt Disney turned that "little fellow" on a drawing pad into a multimillion dollar empire and brought joy to just as many million children and adults, world-wide. They showed us what can happen when we step beyond our usual, customary dimensions of thinking and be willing to stretch. In the world of business, this skill is encouraged, only it goes by a different name:

Problem-solving

Brainstorming
Finding a new use for an old product.
Inventions

If the boss sent around a memo, or announced at a business meeting that he wanted you to "use your imagination" to come up with a solution to the company problem, a lot of you would wonder what on earth he wanted. But, couch the same phenomenon in terms like the above and we know exactly where to head.

It is well known that many of our inventions come from young people. Why? Because they are willing to see the greater picture in their minds. If we allow ourselves to give up preconceived notions that we have about a subject, it is as if we are rising up, out of the walls that bind us in current beliefs, to see a different landscape. There, all manner of things are possible. In this landscape, there is a whole other level to tap into, and kids are undaunted by that. Who else in our society is adept at using their imaginations on a regular basis? Teachers, scientists, medical researchers, writers, poets and artists, hairdressers, and chefs to name a few. If you look at this list, you'll see that they are all creative, the end product of imagining. Is having an active imagination encouraged in our society? No! At a very young age, our journeys into creativity are, sadly, wiped out of us.

"Quit daydreaming, Tommy, get to work."

"Buckle down! Pay attention."

"Trees have to be green. Now tell me, look outside. Do you see any blue trees growing?"

For you readers who are teachers, suppose there is one student in your class that is driving you crazy. Every day there is some argument, a challenging attitude, assignments completed half-heartedly or not at all. At this point, you have the ability to tap into your imagination to find solutions to this dilemma. What is required of you is to not be stuck in the same walls as that student. You have to believe or know the situation can be changed. Otherwise, your imagination or creative solutions will never kick in. You must first quit looking in his direction, for him to change. It will never happen until you allow the possibility that troublesome Tommy can be a productive, positive student. And sometimes, that takes a lot of imagination.

If you feel this kid is a loser and you're stuck with him till the end of the semester, and you dread going to class every day, what message is this sending to your imagination, your creative juices? Will you be lighthearted? No. Of course not. But, as soon as you switch your attitude and say yes, there is a solution to this challenge, you insert that magic key into the doorway to your imagination and, magically, things begin to change. You will change, and so will Tommy. Solutions will come to you. Inventive, new ways to teach. I'm sure you teachers are well aware of the studies documenting this fact. Imagination actually requires a willingness to believe things can be different.

Let's next consider patients with "terminal illnesses," so to speak.

In my practice with four partner-physicians, we rotated on call weekends and would visit all the hospitalized patients for each other, "doing rounds." On one such weekend, I saw Mr. Y., a 70-year-old man suffering from severe emphysema. At the first visit, he lay in his hospital bed, having great difficulty breathing, oxygen mask to his face. His color was bluish instead of a healthy pink and his tearful wife was at his side, holding his hand. After examining him, we talked. His wife, Julie, told me his sons were flying in with their families, one of them with their newest granddaughter, whom Mr. Y. had never seen. Julie wanted so badly for her husband to hang on so he could see this child, and for her sons to be able to say goodbye to their dad. But it looked pretty hopeless.

I asked Mr. Y. if he could last awhile longer, just a couple of days. "Can't you imagine being able to hold that little one in your lap? Picture that. Wouldn't it be wonderful?" I asked him.

"I don't know, Doc," he whispered. "But I'll sure give it a try."

"Great! Just imagine them walking in this door with huge smiles on their faces," I said, and then went off to the nurses' station to write orders for him. I tossed around a lot that night, expecting to receive a call from the nurse, but my telephone was still.

Next morning, back I went to see Mr. Y. He was definitely first on my list. I tiptoed into his room and almost dropped his chart on the floor as I pulled back the curtain. There he was, sitting up in bed, shaving. He had eaten scrambled eggs and ham for breakfast and was now getting cleaned up for the rest of his day. His wife had driven out to the airport to pick up the first of their children. "Hey, Doc! How are ya?" he smiled. "My son's going to be here in two hours and the other one will be here tomorrow, so I figured I'd better get busy. I haven't shaved in a week so this beard is pretty tough."

I was elated. It took me a minute to pull my stethoscope from around my neck, after grinning from ear to ear. As I placed the stethoscope on his chest, I noticed his breathing was easier, his usually erratic, rapid heart had calmed down and his color was pink, not blue-grey. Now here was a man who dug deep inside him, envisioned the best and knew he could accomplish what he yearned for.

Mr. Y. had a wonderful time with his kids, hugged his granddaughter lots, and spent precious time with his wife. Then he slipped peacefully away in his sleep on the third night, his thankful and amazed family surrounding him. We can create miracles using our imaginative powers.

The final story I wish to share with you involved Mrs. M. She was forty years old, in the prime of her life, enjoying a successful career, enthralled with her children, husband and a busy home. Suddenly, one evening, while meeting with her accountant, she was seized with an abdominal pain that almost doubled her over. She wondered at first if it was stress, considering the timing; poring over books of her new business was pretty taxing. But, no, the pain went on, unrelenting. Over the next month of tests and consultations, she learned she had a tumor growing in her pelvis. One of her ovaries had hemorrhaged, fortunately into itself, and had now expanded to the size of a mini-football. Of course, it had to be removed.

At surgery, the surgeon found a small mass attached to one of the walls of the ovary that looked a mite suspicious. He put a little sample on a slide and sent it off to the lab for a quick reading. Fifteen minutes later, the phone rang in the O.R., confirming the diagnosis of cancer, a very rare one at that.

Once Mrs. M. awakened, the doctor entered her room, and stood at the foot of her bed, informing her of the "bad news." Of course this was a shock, and it took a day for her to fully understand. At that point however, Mrs. M. committed to knowing herself as perfectly healthy, visualized going about her business as usual, with ease. Whether it was working at the office, or being wife and mother at home, she saw the same glowing picture.

She chose to undergo conventional treatment, chemotherapy in this case, and to use all the other assistance she could get. As she lay in the hospital once a month for chemotherapy, she put her imagination to work. In the vein dripped the IV chemo, but she saw soldiers routing out the remnants of the enemy cells and destroying them. On another evening, she'd imagine little Pac men, racing through her blood, gobbling up the bad guys. She enlisted the support of her friends, changed her diet, went for walks, played with her family and cut down on stress wherever possible.

It worked.

Today, Mrs. M. is a happy, vibrant lady, cancer-free, who turned her imagined life into reality. She and I are very close, for you see, that lady is me.

Put your imagination to work for you. You do have one. It will manifest in surprising ways. You may find a crazy sense of humor lurking inside; a crafty one, full of innovative ideas; an ability to see a different point of view, the victim's advocate. With imagination, you can turn a fault-finder into a valued company employee. You can perceive what others have omitted, and make a product or service the best in the business. Call upon your imagination, often. You will be astounded and delighted with the changes produced.

J is for Joy

How often do you hear the word 'joy' spoken in today's society? It seems that joy is another concept that is not often voiced, and perhaps seldom felt by a grand part of our population. Joy is a deep-down state. It bubbles to the surface when we are in a simple, uncomplicated place of "being," not "doing."

Look at children. They become joyful as they explore, watch raindrops run down the window; follow the path of a slug across a sidewalk on a rainy day. They are entranced, until we holler, "DON'T touch that slimy thing! UGH!" As children make discoveries, they don't realize it may not be news to us. They rush in the front door to share a precious bit of new information and joy is written all over their face. Recently I read a delightful tale in Reader's Digest, where a little boy had been looking at his birth certificate for the first time, at age seven. He shouted to his mother, "Look. I was born on the same date as my birthday!"

That statement brought joy to both him and his mom, I am sure.

People in so-called third-world countries, in spite of what we would term 'poverty,' experience joy daily. In interviews with Peace Corp volunteers, missionaries, foreign aid employees, the common discovery is that it takes very little to bring forth a huge smile on the faces of the residents of these countries. They experience joy in the daily accomplishment of tasks well done; in simple games they have devised; in learning one sentence in another language. They live in the now. They don't need the latest model car, refrigerator, designer clothing or a two-carat diamond to feel joy.

Ollie Bodtcher was a nurse to a village in Africa several years ago. One of the most frequent requests we received in our young people's group was for used Christmas cards. We would meet one Friday after the Christmas holiday season, and tear off the front of the card. Then, off in the mail would go a huge sack of them to Ollie.

A month later a letter from Africa would arrive, addressed to our youth group. The local natives were absolutely thrilled with the package of card fronts. They would pick their favorites at their youth meeting. Some would be turned into a present for another. Some would be framed to hang on their hut wall. Others would leave the pictures just as they were, to be a treasure for themselves. I learned:

Simple = joy; Heartfelt = joy; Being = joy

Things = want more; More things = craving/ hoarding; More craving = less joy.

I don't need to tell you how to recognize a joyful person. Some have that gleam in their eyes. Others seem to shine with some inner radiance. They sport a contentment you can tune in on. A joyful spirit bounces in your back door with a plate of hot homemade cookies, with nothing expected in return. We can feel joy being out in nature. You can experience joy in a sudden intimate moment when your loved one brushes past you and touches your arm. We can shed tears of joy at the birth of our child or grandchild. It stirs within us as we are caught up in haunting sounds of music.

Joy is contagious. On a trip to Mazatlan last Christmas, we walked along the beach to town, one beautiful afternoon. The sun sparkled on the water, sailboats drifted past. We spied one family on the beach, all of them throwing piles of sand over what appeared to be the oldest child. He giggled. He obviously wasn't worried about how much sand was getting in which orifice of his body, or how long it would take to get it all out of his hair. In fact, he wasn't worried about any consequences, but instead was caught up in the joy of the moment. So was his family, and so were we. We chuckled too as we sauntered by, sharing their laughter, feeling the grains of sand moosh between our toes.

On their website, spiritualityandpractice.com, Frederic and MaryAnn Brussat remind us that joy is just that, a practice. "Joy grows out of faith, grace, gratitude, hope and love. It is our elated response to feelings of happiness, experiences of pleasure, and awareness of abundance."

And now for some of my favorite quotes from writers through the ages. Note the dates on which they were penned.

This is the true joy in life, the being used for a purpose recognized by yourself as a mighty one; the being thoroughly worn out before you are thrown on the scrap heap; the being a force of Nature instead of a feverish selfish little clod of ailments and grievances complaining that the world will not devote itself to making you happy.
George Bernard Shaw (1856 - 1950), *Man and Superman, Epistle Dedicatory*

Joy is prayer - Joy is strength - Joy is love - Joy is a net of love by which you can catch souls.
Mother Teresa (1910-1997)

Short is the joy that guilty pleasure brings.
Euripides (484 BC - 406 BC)

Joy is not in things; it is in us.
Richard Wagner (1813-1883)

Joy is deep, yet bubbles upward. Joy can be solitary or shared. Joy is individual and intimate. It is sourced in simplicity, yet can have profound effects. No one can give joy to another, nor can anyone rob it from you. May deep and lasting joy be yours to recognize, to own, then to share with another.

K: Kiss your Past Goodbye

Steve was a tall man, forty-seven years old, father of two rambunctious boys. He excelled as an accountant. Somehow his mind could micro-manage those numbers, manipulate and massage them into perfect position on the page, make sense of it all and balance the world with his pencil. He was thoroughly capable, but had often failed to venture into his own business, because of his poor self-esteem. He had not done well in school, often took off to hide out with friends in the rough wood clubhouse they built underneath the bridge three blocks away. Steve's mother had remarried when he was seven, no notice, no discussion. No leading up to it, or taking him into her confidence.

"This is your new father," she'd told Steve one morning as he sat up at the kitchen counter eating cornflakes. And just as suddenly, his mother had instructed him to call this man, this stranger in their home, "Dad."

He had choked on that last spoonful and jumped abruptly down to the cold linoleum floor. "What do you mean, my father?" he'd cried. "My daddy died, that's not my dad," pointing his shaking finger at the hulk of a man swilling down a last mouthful of coffee. The guy had just shrugged and muttered, "Whatever, kid."

All the years since that moment, Steve had carried that painful memory someplace deep inside him. Carried it through grade school, where he had to repeat grade five, for too many absences; through run-ins with the police; and flunking out of high school. He'd done everything he could to erase the memory, blot out the pain of that pronouncement in the kitchen on that icy November morning.

He drifted from job to job for years: waiter, construction helper, and dog sitter. (He'd liked that one. At least he could trust animals.) Nothing really stimulated his mind, captured his heart or gave him any sense of self-satisfaction at the end of the day.

Joy? Steve didn't know the meaning of the word.

His motto as he sat at a restaurant one morning, taking reservations, was "Who cares?" Just as he had done when he bathed schnauzers, or ratcheted down loads on a truck, he'd mutter, "So what? I'll never make it. I'll never get what I want."

"Nobody cares what I think," was the big one. For this reason, he never ventured an opinion. Although he was very inventive and thought up clever ideas for improving production or marketing, he seldom spoke up.

One day in 1988, Steve attended a meeting at the coaxing of his girlfriend. Somehow Shelley's gentle nature had allowed him to trust her, as much as he'd ever let himself trust anyone, that is. Skeptical Steve sat in that gathering and wondered initially how he'd ever let himself be talked into what he termed "fairyland, foofoo stuff" about loving yourself. But some inner voice told him to sit in his seat and pay attention. That, plus Shelley's small hand resting so comfortably in his, compelled him to stay. It was the first time he ever recognized how much the past had affected his jobs, his relationships and his self-worth.

Steve began to hang out with these folks, who delighted in his crazy sense of humor. He began to blossom and walk a little prouder, as his talents were recognized and appreciated by others. Steve was finally able to kiss that painful past goodbye. No longer was he the terrified seven-year-old, standing on that cold linoleum floor, feeling worthless and unwanted. He learned in that seminar that he could put his past to rest and look towards a bright future.

Finally, at the restaurant, where his boss had good-naturedly teased him yet trusted him, he began to shine. He made more tips than the rest of the waiters, began coming in early to do the reservations, suggested a change to one item on the menu that brought raves from customers. One day, his boss beckoned to him, "Hey, kid, come in here. Why don't you start doing the books? I don't know nothin' about this stuff. How about it?" As Steve had stood in the doorway, wiping his hands, a puzzled frown on his face, his boss had rattled on, "I'll send you to accountin' school, don't worry about it."

And so, Steve grew into the funny, creative, supportive and talented man he was and had just not recognized before. He discovered his gift with numbers, his ability to organize, his patience and persistence with stubborn books that customers would throw across the room. He discovered he could love and be loved, that he could be a good father, one his children could put their faith in.

Today, as Steve sits in front of me in my exam room, he asks pertinent questions about his health. He tousles the hair of his red-headed twins and grins. I see before me a man who embraces life with his whole self, not holding back He has learned to care, that it's OK, that he matters. He knows he's capable.

I shake his hand. "Steve, we've been together since you were a rebellious fifteen-year-old. You have come such a long way."

"Yeah, Doc," he smiles, "and I start my dream accounting job tomorrow."

We've talked about kissing the past goodbye. How can we go about throwing our arms wide to the future? I mean, practically, really? None of this airy-fairy stuff.

One of the most important facets I've learned over the years of my search is to focus on the goals, the dreams that drive me, and how I want to feel when I reach those goals. I learned not to focus on my undesirable life situation and how I might escape it. A person can develop a horrible wrenched neck or a painful foot, from facing one direction and gawking at their past. Conjures up a pretzel-like image doesn't it? Just as we could not perform this physical feat, so we cannot sustain it with our emotional or mental bodies, nor should we. It is totally self-destructive and limits us from reaching any of our dreams.

When tempted to return to old patterns, envision yourself gazing at the situation you detest, or simply no longer desire in your life, then turn on your heels and look at your dream instead. Go for it, full steam ahead.

There are two different energies here. "Running away from" sucks energy from you. You want to choose the path that increases your energy, makes you go to bed happy and wake up refreshed, keeps you lighthearted. Sometimes this life-change involves a few false starts, a jumping of the gun. That's okay. You can still win the gold. But you cannot do it by running backwards around the track. It takes determination, the ability to say to ourselves, "Yes. I am going to do this."

Epictetus, (55 A.D -135 A.D.) a very wise Roman slave who fulfilled his dream and became a Stoic philosopher, said, "First say to yourself what you would be, then do what you have to do." Now that you have turned your back on what you don't want, answer this question: What have I always dreamed of being or doing?

Say Yes to the goal that tore through your mind when you read that question. As you read earlier in this book, you may have been chased by ghosts from your past, phantoms who whispered, "You could never do that!" Say yes anyway. Turn your back on obnoxious human beings. You know, the ones who spout words like, "*You'll never amount to anything. You're a boy. Boys don't dance. (Or sing, or paint, or...) What are you, some kind of sissy? Who do you think you are, dreaming up such nonsense? You'll never make any money doing that."* Usually this one's accompanied by a sneer. "*You've got to get a real job."*

"*What do you want to get an education for anyways? You need to stay right here at home and help me with these kids. Work on the farm. Help me in the shop."* Whatever.

You're going to have to reach past those ghosts and snatch up your dream or goal. I don't care if you're eighty years old. It is never too late. (Remember my friend, Bill Butler from *A is for Attitude*.)

When I was eleven years old, tropical fish surrounded me. Everywhere you turned in our house were hundreds of these colorful creatures, housed in tanks of all sizes, on every available, conceivable surface, in every room. Both the containers and the shelves had been lovingly crafted by my Dad, for this was his passion, you see. I was enchanted with their patterns, designs, and feeding habits and carried away by the magnificent array of fluorescent colors.

I wrote a little story about several types of these fish, especially personal favorites, the angelfish and neon tetras, and submitted my few paragraphs, complete with pen-and-ink illustrations, to our city newspaper.

Lo and behold, a week or two later, my mother came running into my room. She carried the newspaper in her outstretched hand. "Margaret, when did you do this?" she asked in amazement. "I never even knew you sent it in. This is great, dear!" That was my first published piece. Those fish were so wondrous to me that I wanted to share them with the world. Pure and simple. That passion was there, the dream was mine and I wanted to share it with everyone.

Larger passions loomed however, and writing was pushed into the background as I opted for medical school instead. Very arduous it was, leaving room for little else in life. But over the last few years, the realization that I must leave traditional Medicine became a committed decision, and I faced a new goal. That desire to write made itself known to me anew.

I did a lot of soul-searching and began to focus on my dream that had gathered dust in the corner. I could sit with pen and paper, or pound away at the keyboard for hours, sometimes never even thinking about eating (that was a miracle for me, who loved to munch on cookies or anything chocolate!) I came away from each session energized. Once I shifted to following that dream of writing, the path became easy. Avenues opened up, almost like magic.

I participated in writing workshops to advance that aspect of my dream. One writing class was by correspondence, which was wonderful. I could do it on my own time, from home, clothed or not. The tutor was experienced, professional, yet kind to this vulnerable novice. Then, with the advent of the computer, whole new worlds of online courses became available. Visits to the library offered a free afternoon's outing, as well as a jaunt to explore my avenues more fully. Mostly, I followed my heart, focused ahead on what I wanted.

During this period, a printed piece made a huge impact on my life. A tiny book by Marelin the Magician (the author's name) grabbed my attention. I read *Merlin's Message* over and over.

Sometimes I'd catch myself slipping into old habits. Then I'd grab Marelin's book, peruse a chapter or two, and head back in the right direction. In easy-to-read pages, it packs a powerful message about kissing your passion hello, creating your life the way you want it.

Then, in August of 1998, an article appeared in the Sunday *PARADE* magazine that transformed my life. The article described a lady named Pat Schneider, of Amherst Mass., who led writing workshops for low-income women and children.

With the method she used, as well as persistence and a heap of love, her writers have all left low-income housing. Delinquency rates plummeted, school grades soared and young people in trouble gained the courage to leave gangs behind. Some of them became the first ever in their families to graduate from high school. As I scanned the words in that Sunday paper, I felt my heart lurch. I knew this was what I longed to do, and I knew it with a certainty I hadn't felt since I had chosen to become a physician twenty-eight years previously. Right then, I contacted Pat, took some of her workshops for adults, and then trekked to Amherst to be trained in her method for underserved populations and other topics.

I could have looked back in my life to times I didn't succeed, the rejection letters I'd opened, an earlier divorce, and labeled myself unworthy. I could have listened to the voice that said, "Just stick to being a Doctor, you can't write. You don't have enough training." Instead I chose to go for what my heart knew I could do and was to do.

A year later, you would have found me facilitating Creative writing workshops in Phoenix.

I adore this work, and so do the participants. Several of them have been published. M.A.Hugger is just completing a children's book, *Danny Malloy and his Mississippi Samurai*. Jackie Marx has had several plays produced. She is an amazing creative writer as well as playwright. Yet another woman was angry, about to give up on writing. Her past experience was dictating to her until she discovered her prowess and love of poetry. Miriam Hollingshead has now composed a stunning book of poems entitled *Senior Menu*, dedicated to those with Alzheimer's disease.

Ask yourself this: What gives me such a drive? What gets my blood stirring? Whatever it is, just jump in. Remember Steve. Remember who you are. Kiss your past goodbye, be sure to thank it, and move forward with a large, delicious smooch on the cheek of your kissable future.

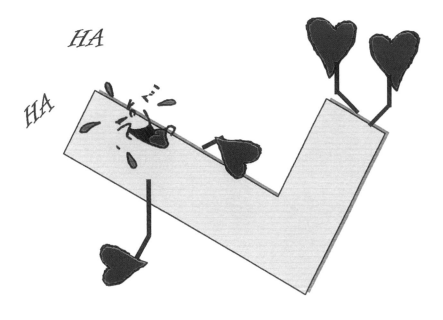

L is for Laughter

A merry heart doeth good, like a medicine
Proverbs 15:13

Research into the effects of laughter on the physical body began in earnest in the 1970's. It was found that exhilaration and laughter triggered release of neuropeptides into the bloodstream. Neuropeptides are chemical messengers that travel through our bodies, linking our nervous, immune and endocrine systems. The more peptides there are, the better immune proteins are generated, and healthier endocrine pathways abound.

What does this mean to us in a practical sense? Simply this: If we have healthier immune systems, if we are more relaxed and our nervous systems can function properly, then more proteins are available to fight diseases.

Does laughter have other beneficial physical effects? You bet. Muscles relax all over. Some muscles, such as the diaphragms, move up and down more, bringing more oxygen to body cells.

Endorphins, our natural analgesics, are released from the brain in huge amounts. If laughter is sustained, the amount of endorphins released is greater than that in runners. William Fry, a pioneer in laughter research at Stanford University says that one hundred belly laughs a day equal the aerobic value of ten minutes on a rowing machine. Laughter burns calories, hour for hour, more than exercise does. Circulation is increased. Our heart speeds up and sends more blood to all parts of our body. Even to our cheeks. Why else do they turn red when we laugh hysterically? More importantly, circulation to our own heart is improved.

There have been several studies done on patients with heart disease, one at the University of Maryland Cardiology Department and another at the UC, Irvine. At the U of M., researchers discovered that patients with heart disease were 40% less likely to laugh in humorous situations. And at UC, forty-eight heart attack patients were studied. Half of them were shown comedy videos each day while hospitalized, the other half were not.

The importance of laughter was also stressed to them in their continuing rehab programs. After one year, ten of the control group had had recurrent myocardial infarcts (heart attacks) compared to only two of the group with humor incorporated daily.

Mentally and emotionally, of course, laughter has beneficial effects. It has been proven that humor makes you more efficient. We are able to think more clearly, increasing productivity. We become much more creative, artistically as well as in problem-solving. Wise business managers know this, and use it.

"Laughter is the most potent, constructive force for diffusing business tension," says Mark H. McCormick, a premier sports business manager and author of *"What They don't Teach You at Harvard Business School."*

Norman Cousins (1912-1990) the former editor of the Saturday Review, was also an articulate advocate in the field of psychoneuro-immunology. In other words, he knew that our psyche, our nervous systems and our immunity to disease were linked. He had proven it in his own life, as he self-treated severe Ankylosing Spondylitis with daily doses of comedy. He said, "Laughter is a form of internal jogging. It moves your internal organs around. It is an igniter of great expectations."

He credits his recovery to laughter and to taking charge of his condition. A month earlier, he had been staring death in the face. He stated, "Death is not the enemy. Living in fear of it is."

Norman Cousins authored an epic book, titled *"Anatomy of an Illness"* which details his experience and his hope.

In my own life I have seen the power of laughter. My hubby, Ron, had a lightning quick sense of humor. We depended on that laughter to fight off pancreatic cancer that thought it was going to take over his body. At first diagnosis, Ron was in the hospital almost a month, undergoing extensive surgery, with a few complications thrown in. In the ICU, barely four hours after the removal of his pancreas, spleen, gall bladder, half his stomach and a section of duodenum, and in severe pain, he joshed with the surgeon, "Hey, did you find any fat in there?"

"Well, very little," the doctor replied.

"Did you take it out?" Ron went on. "I should have slipped you a fifty under the gurney, to do that," he said with a little smile. The surgeon stood at the end of the bed with his mouth agape, totally amazed.

He caught on real quickly though and quipped right back, "Yes, I transplanted it, right here," pointing to his head. Then he left the room, grinning and shaking his head. My sick husband had made that surgeon's day. I like to think that his next operation went a little easier because of that brief encounter with Ron.

In my practice, especially the last few years, I learned that it was perfectly okay to laugh with my patients. They went away feeling so much better even without medications. Meet Bob. A big burly man, with a happy heart, he came to the office, bent over in obvious pain. "Hey, Doc, I passed this an hour ago. You told me to bring it in, so we could analyze it." So saying, he took a tiny piece of gray-toned gravel (a kidney stone) out of a zip-lock bag and sat it on the desk. At that moment, his hand hit the table and the stone bounced off, landing on my carpet, a textured carpet with a mottled pattern, gray-purple in color. "Oh, no!" he exclaimed.

We both stared intently at the floor, willing that tiny stone to reveal itself. Gingerly, I bent down and felt around with my hand. No such luck. We didn't want to stand right away because we didn't want to crush the tiny speck. Pretty soon however, both of us were down on the floor in the exam room on our knees, running our hands over the surface of that carpet, like a mine sweeper.

After about five minutes of this, we suddenly sat up and burst out laughing as we imagined how silly we must look. My nurse knocked on the door and entered to see us still on the floor, sitting back on our heels, with tears of laughter streaming down our faces.

Bob pulled himself up, shook himself off and said, "Well, Doc, I feel just fine now. I'm gonna go home and drink a lot of fluids. If you ever find that damn thing, let me know!"

A patient who had entered the room thirty minutes previously, worried and in agony, left feeling great and chuckling uncontrollably.

Those of us who own or manage an office, can do much to create a happier workplace. Here are a few simple things you could implement in your worksite:

1. Institute joke- of- the- day boards.
2. Have humor contests.
3. Sponsor a night out at a comedy club.
4. Hire a fun, motivational speaker for a lunch-hour talk.
5. Post cartoons.
6. Have a fun half-day for the whole group.
7. Sign a personal contract for play. Set goals for yourself and keep them!

What are the beneficial "side effects" for you?

First of all you'll feel better, sleep better, handle stress with more ease. As the atmosphere in your work arena lightens up, so will you. In fact, some days, you'll feel you didn't even have any stress.

There will be fewer complaints from employees and customers. Clients will think the service has improved just because you and your staff are happier. You'll find employees more cooperative, and eager to be a team player. Remember too, they and you will be more creative and solve challenges more quickly.

Your business will increase. Who wants to refer others to an old grouch?

For the rest of us, I encourage you to recall these stories when you are in a stressful situation. Prescribe a chuckle an hour, or minute by minute, if necessary, and get those hormones flowing. Take a taste of your own new brand of "medicine." Remember, it is more effective in multiple doses.

M is for Magic

Magic:

1. The art of producing a desired result through the use of various techniques
2. Any extraordinary or irresistible influence, charm, power

   E.g.   The magic of spring

   A magical moment

   The magic of music

3. Mysteriously enchanting

Remember the song, *Magic Moments*? How many times did you sing or whistle along with Perry Como on that one?

♪ *Magic moments, mem'ries we've been sharing*

Magic moments, when two hearts are carin'   ♫

Time can't erase the memory of

♫ *These magic moments filled with love.*

Hal David and Burt Bacharach had it right, almost fifty years ago. We never do forget magical moments that enrich our lives.

Let me say right here that I do not speak of black magic, evil curses, spells, sorcery and the like. To me these are a form of control over others and most often do not leave a person feeling carefree and joyful. Certainly, I have been vastly entertained by a magician and left that theater in awe. Or, many of us have had a good laugh over parlor games, but I'll leave those activities for another book.

In my medical practice and experience, I have witnessed or experienced first-hand several instances of magic. Or perhaps, miracles would describe these events more accurately. Whatever term you use, looking for magic in my life makes it more fun. The little child still there inside me, can jump up and down and clap her hands.

For instance, at one point in Medical school, I became very despondent. Life seemed nothing but books, tests, books and work, work, work. I hadn't had a day off in over three weeks, Biochemistry midterms were looming close by; a horrible bout of bronchitis made me feel like throwing all my efforts out the second story window; and my boyfriend and I had just split up.

I lay in bed one evening, feeling very sorry for myself. I stared at the dull ceiling of peeling paint and thought, *You know, you could lie here dead for three days and no one would even miss you.*

Sobering reflection, but probably true, because everyone knew of my busy schedule and wouldn't worry if I didn't call for a while. Out of the blue, another voice boomed in my head, *Do you think everyone on earth is put here to make little Margaret happy?*

Well, no…

You're right, the voice continued, *It's up to you to be happy.*

That was one magical moment. I looked at life, relationships and myself very differently from that point on. I remember it as clearly now, as if it had just happened last night. A few minutes after that experience, the phone rang in my tiny apartment. It was my friend, Gail, who lived miles away on Vancouver Island. I hadn't seen her for years, nor had we talked for at least one year.

"I was worried about you," she said, "and I wanted to make sure you are okay. Something told me I should call you. Are you all right?"

Gail and I talked that evening for hours, catching up on each other's news, laughing over old dates we'd had, and crazy fun at church cookouts. When we said goodbye, I felt so much better. How had she known to call at that exact moment? Moreover, what if she hadn't?

I learned to look for magic, allow it in my life. Gail also taught me the power and value there is in reaching out to others. Writing a card, telling someone a sincere Thank You, making that telephone call. We can be a healing magician in another person's life, as well as our own.

We can use this attitude of "magic" to stave off illness. My friend, Sandy, traveled with me recently to a writers' conference in California. The second morning there, she awoke with fever, chills, and was coughing up blood. As a physician, I was horrified. But Sandy said, "Don't worry, I've had this before, it's this pollution in the air. I just meditate and it goes away."

Sure enough, three hours later, she walked into the classroom, ready to go. No more fever, no chills, no blood or cough.

There have been times when I was too busy to let myself be ill. Patients to see in the hospital, babies to deliver, a vacation upcoming, four kids, bills to pay and costumes to sew. I'd feel the flu coming on or some other malady attempting to push its way into my body. (Actually, I realized later in life that it was my body warning me. Go to bed and rest, you idiot!) But I said No to the disease. I sometimes talked out loud, "I don't have time to deal with you. Now get out of here and leave me alone." It worked many times, my own style of magic.

I am sure that you have heard stories or experienced your own form of magic in your life, but perhaps you'd forgotten those times until now.

Running into an old friend at the mall for example, someone you'd wished you could talk to and didn't know how to reach. Being introduced to exactly the person you needed to meet for a business deal, a new friendship, tutoring, etc. Unexpected money falling into your hands. Being saved from a car mowing you down, as you stepped off a curb. Having surgery cancelled at the last moment because a mass in your liver, or lung or brain had totally disappeared. How about someone giving up their seat on an airplane so that you could make that emergency trip home. Isn't that magical?

I encourage you to take a few minutes over the next week and list the magic that has happened in your life. Those happy events, long- forgotten and sometimes, not even acknowledged or recognized with thanks. If you like, use the next page to recreate magic moments.

Look for magic in your life. Help to create it for others. Wave your wand. Lift your spirits.

MY MAGIC MOMENTS:

Remember when: What I'd like to see now:
  1.   1.

  2.   2.

  3.   3.

  4.   4.

  5.   5.

  6.   6.

  7.   7.

  8.   8.

  9.   9

  10.   10.

N is for Naughty or Nice

Raised in late 19th century England, in a home where Daddy was a traveling preacher and Mum was "Mother," not Mummy, Annie learned the rules of etiquette and proper behavior at a very young age. By the age of five, she'd felt the sting of a ruler across her outstretched hand. And by that same age, she'd completed grade one in the tiny two-room schoolhouse down the village lane. By the age of eight, Annie had become a rascal and a rebel. Somehow the laughter of her school chums was more enticing than buckling down with pen and paper at her wooden desk, to do her "sums."

On more than one occasion, she would finish her work early, then stare around for something else to do. She'd sit back in her seat and yawn loudly at first. If that didn't garner enough attention from the students in each row beside her, she'd grab one pigtail of Lucy, who sat in front of Annie, and dip it in the inkwell at the top of her desk. All of these activities were accompanied by winks and twitches and quiet humming on Annie's part, plus increasingly loud snickers and wide grins from her classmates. Finally the activity at the back of the room became raucous enough to catch the stern eye of Miss Grimsby, the teacher, who had been busy at her desk, doing teacherly things like grading papers with a threatening red pencil.

One bright, crisp winter morning Annie realized that the room had suddenly become very dark indeed. Glancing to her side, Annie saw sturdy black laced-up boots, a long tightly knitted skirt, topped by a purple blouse. It was buttoned so tight to Miss Grimsby's throat that her neck puckered and gave her face the color of ripe Bing cherries. Annie was marched to the front of the classroom, propelled there by the teacher's bony fingers locked onto Annie's collar. There she was made to stand at attention in front of her fellow students. "You will stand behind the chalkboard for fifteen minutes, Miss Booth," the teacher shrieked. "And no noise out of you. Do you understand me?"

"Oh, yes, Miss Grimsby," Annie's eyes lowered appropriately and ever so briefly, in feigned submission. The class was still. Not one foot shuffled, no one shifted in their seats. All of the students stared at Miss Grimsby, their straight starched uniforms in rows, like blue penguins at attention. Suddenly, Miss Grimsby heard a giggle, then mutters, a chuckle, saw laughter stifled behind hands. She wondered who could be the cause now. If she had looked down, she would have seen Annie stretched out flat on the floor beneath the chalkboard.

She lay next to the teacher, with tongue out and cheeks pulled stiffly back, eyes crossed and panting. Tiny white puffs of air escaped into the chilly classroom and danced across the tops of Miss Grimsby's unsuspecting boots. Just then the bell rang, ending the period. Annie jumped to her feet, brushed the dust off her skirt and poked her head around the chalkboard. "May I leave now, Miss?" she asked, ever so politely.

"Yes, yes, Annie. Gather up your things quietly and be gone with you. No nonsense like this tomorrow, Annie, or I will have to report you."

"Yes, Miss Grimsby. Thank you," and off she darted back to her desk to grab her books.

Such antics and fun-loving attitude enabled Annie to make it through World War I, train to be a nurse and serve through World War II, move to America, become a mother at age forty-two and raise a mentally-handicapped daughter, as well as two other daughters. A second career found Annie in front of a classroom herself. The same naughty ploys that carried her through her school years, now came into play as she cajoled and convinced her young charges to study.

Books raised to eye level and supposedly following Annie's lead, each student was to repeat sentences from their reader after Annie read them once. At one point, Annie suspected they weren't paying attention at all, and so she said, "And Moses dug potatoes." The errant children echoed back, "And Moses dug potatoes." Amidst much coughing and giggles, they quickly realized their error and stammered or stuttered the proper words. Annie suppressed her grin behind her textbook but I am sure her twinkling eyes gave her away that day. Perhaps she traveled back in time to remember a girl named Lucy, who walked home many times from school, crying because of ink-sodden pigtails. And for sure she remembered well who the perpetrator was.

Fortunately, for those who knew Annie, she developed another part of her that became nice: caring, tender, loving, forgiving, and thoughtful. These attitudes and ways of being, kept her lighthearted, positive and hopeful through the most difficult years of her life.

She was also one of the most creative persons I have known. The same spirit of naughtiness stimulated a curiosity of things unknown and untried. She took up weaving. I remember visiting her tiny abode, and seeing a large loom in her dining room. She created the most beautiful rugs, but was never one to brag about such things. She cut hair, taught Sunday school, taught herself to high-dive at age fifty, wrote beautiful poetry and learned how to make delicious soups. During the Depression years, she made pots of soup every day, and carried them in her arms up the street to the elementary school, to feed the hungry mouths of children whose parents had fallen on tough times.

Annie gifted us with a wonderful legacy, a shining example of how to live, really live life, whether she was being naughty or nice. She was my grandmother.

O is for Outrageous

...and I said, "You can stop, if you want, with the Z
Because most people stop with the Z, but not me!
In the places I go there are things that I see
That I never could spell if I stopped with the Z.
On Beyond Zebra,
Theodor Seuss Geisel, 1955

Puss approached the ogre's tower. At its tip-top, the filthy
ogre was burping and snorting over his disgusting dinner...
"Ogre, be a lion!" Puss yelled. A huge angry lion with cruel claws and terrible teeth,
appeared and roared so loud that the cat's fur stood up straight, his tail a ramrod.
But Puss managed to meow, "Ogre, be a mouse!" In a flash, the lion
vanished and a tiny mouse scampered across the filthy floor. Puss pounced.
Puss In Boots,
Cesar Cui, 1913 opera

    I don't know about you, but as a child, I reveled in nursery rhymes and fairy tales. I don't remember that I learned any hidden meanings or deeper levels to some of the tales, but do recall my imagination carrying me far away. Impossibility became possible.

    On reviewing *Puss 'N Boots* for this book, I was carried back to those 'Anything is possible' days. Now this Puss was one cool cat! He put on his magic armor, that pair of black leather boots, and could slay dragons, transforming the overwhelming monsters in his life into mewing, doable, mini-mice. He simply waved his magic wand and he was in charge, not cowering or afraid to move on. Puss was outrageous!

What does 'outrageous' mean to you? For Kathy, a fifty-six year old patient, it was having the courage to go to a movie by herself. You may scoff, but for her, it was a big deal. And to eat dinner out in a top-notch restaurant was the supreme challenge. Especially the ones where she stood at the desk and the maitre d' would ask, "Just one?" The ultimate admission of aloneness, those solo movies and dinners, yet as she did it more often, she related on one follow-up office visit, she actually came to enjoy the experience.

Being outrageous means different things to different people. Take Tom, for instance. He was the epitome of gregariousness, the life of the party as he flitted from one pretty face to another, drink in hand. Glad-handing the men, the friendly slap on the back. Always moving. Great guy. For Tom however, being outrageous meant taking a hike in the woods with his best buddy, Ken. Sitting by a river, quiet, still, perhaps not even fishing, just being there, that was a real stretch for him. Several times in the first horrid twenty-four hours, he had to forcibly keep himself there. It was a test of honor to remain at the campsite and not bail out on his buddy. He learned to decipher footprints in the ground, became fascinated with the caws of blackbirds, tied a perfect fly for fly fishing, mastered the art of throwing that line just so, and even caught fish.

Tom found that when he did force himself to simply be there and actually learn to enjoy his foray into the wilderness, that he always returned to work and home, feeling like he'd shed ten pounds, emotionally and physically.

Several years ago, before Ron and I got together, I dated a fellow whose passion was dune buggies. It was a thrill for him to careen up, down and over those sand dunes at top speed. One sunny weekend, my mother and I accompanied Mark to the dunes just outside Yuma, AZ. That day, my seventy-six year-old mother was the outrageous one.

She had just recently recovered from massive abdominal surgery. So, as she stepped over the rails of that strange vehicle and we strapped her in, I reassured her. "Don't worry, Mom. He promised me he'd take it easy. He'll just take you for a nice little ride over there," I said, pointing to a gentle slope. Waving goodbye and trusting Mark completely, off she went for her "nice little ride." However, the words, "being nice, little, just, gentle, and promise" were foreign to Mark.

In a few minutes, as I searched for them in the crowds of buggies on the hill, I stood, horrified, my hand over my mouth. "Oh, no," I screamed. "What is he doing?"

For there were Mark and my mom barreling down one of the steepest dunes in the place, bouncing up and down, side to side. Finally she screamed for him to stop, as her poor abdomen was being tossed all over, causing her much pain. I could see her holding her tummy with one hand and whacking him with the other.

However, as they pulled to a stop in front of me, she was grinning. Mom had never learned to drive a car. She had chickened out on her second lesson with my Dad, after she steered their car into a ditch. Yet, at seventy-six, she had placed herself in the hands of this wild, racing, no-holds-barred dune buggy fanatic. Now that's outrageous!

It seems to me that being outrageous means facing and overcoming our own personal demons; taking the step beyond what we thought possible; or beyond the limits that others so carefully had constructed on our behalf; doing what others said would never work. Yet we accomplished it in spades.

John, a delightful patient, had developed a serious eye condition, retinitis pigmentosa, which rendered him blind by the age of thirty. Now, at forty-two, he visited my office with Luke, his loyal guide dog, to say goodbye. John and his wife had been patients for about five years and were now moving to Colorado, so that he could attend law school. They had been in to have me sign papers so that the university would purchase him a Braille computer. I could imagine how difficult it would be to move to a new home, learn to maneuver around a new apartment, and cope with the daily tasks that the sighted community takes so much for granted.

Any wimpy person would have said, "No way." But not John, nor his wife, Linda. Even Luke sported a bright red leash, a symbol of their outrageous attitude. He left the office with his tail wagging. John, Linda and I hugged and shed tears. I admire that couple so much.

Way before he was my husband, Ron moved to Hawaii and dared to open the first Mexican restaurant in Waikiki. Situated on Kalakaua Avenue, the main drag, full of Hawaiian restaurants, huge hotels, luaus and lei stands, business acquaintances told him he'd lose his shirt. Bankers sat behind their desks, looked at him like he was crazy, and shook their heads, "No!" All that is, except one, who caught the spark of Ron's visionary fire, and the two struck up a very lucrative partnership.

Wise thing too. That establishment was a huge success. Ron rented three rooms upstairs, tore down walls, redecorated it in a Mexican theme, and stayed open all night. He hired the best musicians and great cooks. He put tables on the balcony overlooking the street and instantly the place was booming. Tourists as well as locals, made it their favorite spot to hang out. They could devour Mexican food in an Aloha shirt, no problem.

If you know inside that something is possible, be unstoppable, and go for it. Turn that fearsome lion into an edible mouse. Don't be afraid to be a Puss!

P is for Passion

P: Purpose
A: All-encompassing
S: Seductive, draws you in, even when you know you should be ironing, studying, resting, cooking dinner
S: Sees no obstacles, only opportunities
I: Inspiring. Increased energy, zest for life
O: Overcoming, ongoing
N: New each day

When I lived in Honolulu, Hawaii, I read an ad in the Saturday paper, inviting all those interested to come to the park on Sunday morning to enroll in training for the annual marathon. So began a great adventure, one that would teach me every aspect of this idea of passion. I began with the purpose of losing weight and getting my body into good shape. I sagged in all the wrong places and anyone looking for love, looked right past me. Besides, I wanted to take on that challenge, to complete something that seemed such a stretch, do something I never thought I could. As the weeks passed, that marathon became more seductive. I certainly had more energy, enthusiasm, and needed less sleep. I overcame my doubts, my terrible physical condition, and my poor image of self. I made some lifelong friendships. What had begun as a good idea, quickly turned into a passion for me.

Marathon Day arrived. Imagine hundreds of people gathered in the park, milling around the starter's box, anxious for the race to begin. For me, all I wanted to do was to complete the 26.2 miles. That would be sweet victory. Many of us had become comrades in this quest. Now we grinned, gave each other high-fives, words of last-minute encouragement, "Yes! Of course you can do it." What a time that was.

But about the thirteenth mile, I developed a severe pain down the side of my right leg. Pretty soon, it became excruciating. No matter which way I turned my body, how fast or slowly I ran, the pain wouldn't leave. I had to slow to a walk, and then almost a crawl. By then, all the other runners and joggers had passed me by. I struggled on, feeling more and more defeated by the yard. All my dreams for naught.

Suddenly, as I limped sadly along, I heard a swishing noise behind me. I turned to see three marathoners approaching. They came whizzing down the hill behind me, their strong arms pushing, pumping. They gulped huge breaths of air, and sported the biggest smiles I had ever seen. Immediately my sadness evaporated, my state of feeling so sorry for myself vanished. For these three men were in wheelchairs. Wheelchairs propelled by people who had no use of their legs. I waved like crazy as they wheeled past. I could see the sweat and the determination written across those faces. "Yes. You can do it!" I hollered.

I never did complete that marathon, but I certainly learned a whole lot about commitment, and even more about passion and joy.

(The author did complete the full marathon, in Alaska, 1998. I took on the cause of raising money for the Leukemia and Lymphoma Society, trained for six months ahead of time, and enrolled many friends in the project. These were my fuel. I was one ecstatic puppy, running in to that finish line.)

Several years later, I was attending a weeklong seminar in San Diego, put on by the Chopra Institute. One evening, I experienced passion in its ultimate form. It came in the person of Malcolm Watson, a master violinist. But Malcolm didn't stand, proper and immobile in the center of the stage. He wasn't clad in a black tuxedo or suit. Instead, he pranced about the stage, leaped off its edge to the auditorium floor, tore down the middle aisle, playing his electric violin all the while. Then he dashed back up the aisle and jumped up onto the stage once again. He was dressed in an immaculate white tuxedo, hot pink bowtie, and bare feet. Longish hair flew out behind him and it danced about as fast as his violin bow. Do you wonder why I remember him after all these years? Besides all this visual freedom, the sounds that came from that violin were the sweetest I have ever heard.

If you had been in the audience that evening, you would have known, as soon as his hands guided the bow across those strings, that Malcolm was transported to a more heavenly place than that room. Beautiful, raucous, bawdy, tender notes sprung from that violin. He was in his glory, and carried us to another world, to experience ours.

That's the beauty of passion: when other people catch a glimpse or glimmer of our passion, they are affected too. They are carried to a place where all things are possible; where hope abounds for any problem; time becomes timeless; and definite lightheartedness reigns supreme.

It was my pleasure to sit with Malcolm at lunch the next day. "But, how did you know that playing the violin was your passion?" I asked. I had been thinking about my two grandsons, and how they would discover their passions in life.

He replied, in his lilting English voice, "For my seventh birthday present, my uncle gave me his prized violin. As soon as I took that bow in my small hands, and laid it across those strings, I knew this was for me. Even at that age, I could feel the music inside me, wanting to pour out." It was easy to see that he'd never given up that passion.

Inspiring? All-encompassing? Definitely.

Passion can take many forms, of course. We can be passionate about a pet, a cause, our grandchildren, our favorite sports team, making the best goat cheese we've ever tasted; swimming naked in an ancient pool in a deserted canyon in Sedona, AZ. We can feel just as enamored, energized, tireless and refreshed about a hobby or pastime, as we do about a lover.

Passion cannot always be reasoned or understood. Often, in the midst of passion, you forget to eat, even forget you're hungry, forget your mate, a date, you're late, you're forty-eight. We can make a fool of ourselves in pursuit of our passion and it is okay.

Passion can also have a quiet, calm, soothing voice of contentment. It doesn't always need to present itself screaming, arm-waving or standing on corners. Just because we've unleashed our passion, doesn't mean we know all there is to know about that field either. Realizing what we've always felt about photography for instance, doesn't mean we can publish our book of Native

American portraits next week. We may need to research, interview, and study the craft of photography as well as the art; travel, buy a new camera, experiment with techniques, invest time and money, establish goals. And then practice, practice, practice.

But all along, it is our passion that will be the fuel to keep us going, the force that won't let the fire go out. All the time we are taking the necessary steps to our dream, time will fly, and miracles will happen.

Malcolm Watson (Xcentric Recordings), and those wheelchair marathoners will always remind me of the awesome results of passion. They are lasting beacons in my life. Go ahead. Let yours loose.

Q is for Question

Indeed, she had quite a long argument with the Lory,
who at last turned sulky, and would only say, 'I am older
than you and must know better.'
Alice's Adventures in Wonderland, Lewis Carroll

Never be afraid to question supposed experts even if they're older than you. Does their advice ring true? Does it fit with your previous experience in a situation? Even if not, look to see where they *might* be right. Ask yourself, "Could there be another approach? This or that worked well for me, can it be used in this current dilemma?"

Find out if the 'expert' has something to gain by sticking adamantly to his or her position. If at work, is there a raise in the offing for them? A bonus if they sell so many doohickeys guaranteed to curl your toenails, and you know they don't work? A promotion? With friends, do they have a point to prove, a need to control you? Or is their expertise garnered from careful study and personal observation? All good questions for you to consider thoughtfully.

One patient, J.S., passed on a wonderful pearl of wisdom, which I've never forgotten. J.S. was a top-notch businessman. He told me that he always followed this ritual with any important decision in his life:

"Reflect on the advice you've been given, or the arrangement you've agreed to, for a day. Before you go to bed, pretend that the choice is made, complete, the papers are signed. Then see how you feel when you waken."

When he shared his tale, he had just signed all but the final papers in a business deal with his partners. That evening, he pretended to himself that it was a 'done deal,' and he went to bed to sleep on it. The next morning, he awakened with nausea, diarrhea and a sinking feeling in his abdomen. He knew right then, that this arrangement was not the perfect one for him. He called his partners for another meeting, discussed his concerns and made new agreements. J.S. had learned the hard way to do this, but once he learned to question and relied on his own internal wisdom, his life changed for the better.

Often, we fear that if we say No to something or somebody that it means that relationship will have to end. Not so. Often it is simply a matter of changing one small facet, a time to meet, a chore, a budget item, for example. How many times has our partner, lover or spouse said, "I hate that ------ on you. What ever possessed you to buy that?" If it happens to be one of our favorite items of clothing, if we feel so comfortable in it, if a special person gave it to us and we love to wear it, guess what? Wear it! But if we choose to wear the dress or shirt because we have an inkling that it will annoy the other person, think again. Ask, will it really hurt for me to wear something different this time? Am I doing this just to annoy them? Take a minute and question yourself.

How many times has another person made a statement to you, or advised a certain course, and you totally take it another way? You quite naturally and innocently grasp one meaning from their statement, while their intent was completely different. Often times, we experience a strange little sensation, like something's not quite right. It never hurts to ask for clarification in these circumstances. Perhaps you missed an item or two in their explanation. Maybe there was no explanation, just control. Find out if the who, why, where, when and how matches your understanding and need. It's much easier to ask beforehand, than to fix a mess after. Don't even question the voice that yells, like the Lory, "Because I said so!" Dismiss that one.

Finally, a good question to ask ourselves intermittently through the span of our lives is this: *What is my soul trying to tell me? What am I here to do, really?*

You met Keith earlier. He is a very robust, vibrant man, content, very willing to experience life to the fullest possible extent. As he shared his experience with me, I listened, questioned and learned. He had written out the following exercise himself and found it to be of great value. Make a list of all the major events of your life. The list is written without editing or self-judgment as to whether the event was "good" or "bad." Whatever pops into your head as a major life event is fine. Review the list to see if there are common threads among some of the activities or happenings.

Which ones brought enjoyment? What did you hate? Learn the most from? Love to do the most? Where did you experience the greatest joy? Which ones involved just you? What events or choices of activities affected others or were conjured up by them?

Ask now: What are these activities or happenings in my past trying to tell me?

Do any "accidents" have to threaten your very earthly existence for you to pay attention? Sandy, a nurse who does house calls for her company, has seen it all. She tells it this way: The first time, the Universe will tap you on the shoulder, to try to wake you up, and look at a particular situation that is not in your best interest. The next time, we may get a harder bop on the head if we don't listen. And after awhile, if we're really stubborn, it may take a serious accident to make us sit up and really take notice.

Sandy knows all this first-hand, as well as from her nursing patients. Ten years ago, her husband had a drinking problem. He didn't recognize it as a problem, but his family and friends did. No amount of personal talk would convince him to cut down his intake of alcohol, let alone stop. One evening, he climbed the stairs to their apartment, missed the last step and fell all the way to the floor below. His children heard an awful bang, then moans and screams. Running out the apartment door, they found him in a heap at the bottom of the stairs. This wonderful husband and dedicated father was paralyzed from the neck down.

Only then did he learn to listen to the small voice inside that had been trying in vain to get his attention. Only then did he pay attention and realize what he had been doing with his life, how it was deviating from his best path. But it was too late.

On a personal level, I learned so much by preparing this 'significant life events' list. When I looked at it honestly, and asked, "What is my soul here to experience in this lifetime?" my breath caught. For there in front of me lay the pattern of my life, my soul's desire to experience certain feelings, circumstances, victories and relationships. The road map and direction for my life was in plain view on that piece of paper. I learned to look honestly and to listen for honest answers.

For example, we might ask ourselves:

Why don't I laugh much any more? What is weighing me down? (Gained weight recently?) Why am I working and expending all my energy on a job I hate? This question is a huge one for many people. When you consider how many hours a day we spend at work, is it any wonder we have sick, disgruntled, exhausted folks, when they hate what they're doing every minute of those hours?

If this describes you, try meditating, pray, watch, write, walk, and get quiet. Ask for the answers to come. They will. Reflect on your past. When was I most happy and fulfilled? What activity was I engaged in at that time? Find the answer, then find or create a job for yourself that you delight in.

Why am I staying married to this spouse? Why am I in this loveless, (abusive, faithless) marriage just because I pledged to a judge whose name I forget, pledged to a man/woman who could care less now, that I'd hang in there "for better or worse?"

So many times I heard patients in my office state, "I know it's bad, but it's better than living all alone." Meanwhile they had ulcers, or shingles, or were beaten up, had gained seventy pounds from all the stress, but they didn't love themselves enough to leave.

Just recently came the following email. It speaks of God's care for us. Whatever your God is called, please read this message with that name in mind.

Eileen Cady is one of the co-founders of the Findhorn community in Scotland. The message she shares is this:

"Be afraid of nothing. It matters not what anyone may think of your actions when you know that what you are doing is done under My guidance and with My blessing. Do it with real joy and see the very best come out of it. Never at any time forget that My ways are not men's ways.

That is why I say that you have to learn to step out fearlessly into the unknown without even a pattern to follow, but with absolute faith and confidence in Me and My ways.

Never do it on just your own strength. I am in the midst of you, uniting, guiding, directing and uplifting you; and in uplifting you I will draw all humanity upwards."

What an inspiration and encouragement. What synchronicity that it should appear on my email right now, as this chapter is being completed.

Be willing to question and listen to the answers. It takes guts and faith. Faith in yourself, and in a loving presence that wants the best for you. Honestly, if you are choosing that which is your highest good, the help will come. Often from amazing, unexpected sources, but it will appear for you. Do this and you will find the heavy load lift, you'll breathe easier, and you will be able to be lighter as you face each new day.

I must add this, in case the reader thinks that all I see are people with huge personal problems. Not so. But so many of us were brought up never to question our parents, our teachers, our priest, rabbi, minister, our counselor, our spouse, that I feel a good healthy dose of honest questioning of our situations can be beneficial for us. And, the answers we come up with may certainly affirm what we are already doing. Wonderful!

R: Rid Your Rooms of Junk

You might ask, how on earth is throwing out junk supposed to make me feel light-hearted? As an example, if you were to wander through my house and garage, you'd realize instantly that it would take me hours of focused labor to sort through all the stuff I have, and that wouldn't make me happy at all. You'll hear me rationalize: Well, a lot of it is required for my job; some of it is a box of games for when the kids and grandkids visit; two boxes I see are labeled "Hobbies." I haven't opened those boxes since I moved in years ago.

Some are very precious family pictures, ten cartons of various and sundry photos from the past twenty eight years. My friend, Judy, and I are planning to get together in a couple of months, to go through all the photos, sort them and eventually create beautiful albums for our family members. (We've been "planning" this for over two years now.) She finally began without me and has sorted hers into piles on her table. I really want to have mine completed before I die. I will never throw those out. You wouldn't really expect me to, would you? But to realize that goal, I must take action.

My question is, I try to stay neat and tidy, but it seems that at least once a week, I arrive home to piles of papers that suddenly stacked up on my dining room table in my absence. How do I prevent this mess?

If you search the Internet for references to decluttering, you will find over 844,000 sites! That's enough to make you shudder and drag the dumpster to your door, isn't it? However, there are really some fun, wise experts to assist you, like Peter Walsh for example. He's appeared on Oprah's show, hosts TLC's *"Clean Sweep"* program, written several books on the subject and even has a handy quiz for you to take online.

I did just that and discovered I was a "clutter victim." Mr. Walsh says it's because I have a busy life, diverse interests, disposable income (I dispose of it very quickly), family memorabilia and a steady influx of purchases and junk mail. He was right on. How could he tell all that about me with just ten simple questions? Very interesting and downright scary.

The good news is that there's hope. Once I develop a system and stick to it, Peter Walsh says I can keep my home clutter under control. Then I can start on my office and car. Whew! His website may be of interest to you. It is www.peterwalsh.com.

Then there is the Zen habits site at www.zenhabits.net. Leo Babauta lives on Guam and writes from there. He recommends tackling one room, one drawer or closet at a time for fifteen minutes a day. Celebrate what you've accomplished and then repeat the next day. Or if you are so inclined, set aside two to four hours on a Saturday morning to clear one room, even a large closet. See how you feel when you're done. Leo says he feels awesome.

I personally think that if we stay focused for that long, some type of endorphin is released from our brain, causing lots of great decluttering vibes.

In Phoenix, we have our own "Queen of Clean," Linda Cobb. She began sharing her vast knowledge of cleaning spots, wax, etc, in her book called *Talking Dirty with the Queen of Clean."* More recently, she authored, *"The Queen of Clean Conquers Clutter,"* which you can find on her handy website.

There are a few maxims that all of these gurus agree on:

1. If you haven't used an item in a year, give it away or throw it out.
2. One In-One Out. If you want to buy that lovely blouse, do it, but you must throw out or give away one item of clothing. Is there a tool you can't live without? Go ahead and purchase it but then choose one you already own and hand it over to your neighbor, Joe. He'll love it and think you're cool.
3. Show no mercy. No emotional attachment.
4. When the Give-Away box is full, stop what you're doing, put the box in your car and drive it to the nearest Thrift shop or Goodwill of your choice.
5. Don't attempt to do too much at once. You'll likely get burned out and not want to do more. Celebrate and have fun after each room, drawer or cupboard is complete.

So, there you have it. It took me a month to actually sit down in the midst of my cluttered computer room/ library/ creative glassworks room/ Christmas tree storage shelves, to find space to lay my arms so as to type this chapter. Is it any wonder it took me so long to gather the courage to pen these words, when my own room is so disorganized?

Now I can pull up my sleeves and get to work on ridding this room of junk, so I can smile again and feel awesome when I walk in here.

S is for Save/Savor

Save a few minutes of each day, just for you, and savor that time. Value, cherish, delight in it and don't allow anyone to rob you of those minutes. They are yours.

Choose which time of day is best for you. Many people find the morning hours suit them while others would find it torture to haul themselves out of bed at such an ungodly hour. This experience would not be savory at all. You'll know.

Use the time to exercise, meditate, read a favorite book, make your list of priorities for the day, or write a letter you've been putting off. Whatever makes you happy and leaves you contented. Or inspired. Notice that the list does not include balancing your bankbook, making a grocery list, paying bills, or ironing your clothes for work. I am talking about pleasurable things here.

Often, those fifteen or twenty minutes will help you become centered and calm in the eye of the storm. Then the rest of your day will fall into place without effort or strain.

Those who meditate or pray in the morning find they are much more productive with higher energy levels if they adapt this regimen faithfully. Studies have shown they require much less sleep as well. I found this out for myself at a seminar recently. Beginning each morning and afternoon with meditation, I was very skeptical as to how productive it would be. I remember whining, "I didn't pay all this money to come here and meditate. I want to learn something."

And learn, I did. At first it was extremely frustrating, as I had to quiet my mind. It kept wanting to chatter away in the background, question, figure it out, think and come up with all sorts of ideas as to what I should be doing right then.

I finally learned to shut off the chatterbox and take that time for me. At the end of just one week, my creativity had increased exponentially. I'd awaken at 3:00 AM, totally refreshed, and write poems. Now this was a new one. At first I didn't understand the urge to pick up my pen. Why was I thinking about lions at this time of the morning? Finally I quit questioning and followed orders. Poems began to pour out of me. Mid-afternoon fatigue that had swamped me previously, vanished in that short week's time. I was happier, creative and bounced through the day, rather than dragging. Huge difference.

If you are one of those people who throw down two cups of coffee with no breakfast between the shower and the front door, consider stopping. You may feel more awake with the caffeine, but consider that this is a short-lived high and a further jolt must be administered in an hour or two. You'll realize this if you begin to pay attention to your body as well as your mind. The benefits of increased production and creativity are yours for the taking, if you give your private time a try.

Some folks are not morning people. They would be better off taking their special time after work or in the evening. Whatever works better for you, do that. If you prefer a twenty-minute jog to working out at the gym, go for it. Don't force yourself to undertake an activity that you don't enjoy simply because your spouse does it, or someone has told you it's good for you.

Studies have shown too, that some individuals are more rested and energized after a nap, and others, after exercise. It took Chloe years to discover this phenomenon for herself. She had always become frustrated when trying to overcome marked fatigue by taking an afternoon snooze. Her friends would zone out within seconds, revived and refreshed after twenty minutes. Not her. She'd get up more tired than ever, and totally frustrated, to boot.

Finally, once we'd discussed an article addressing this issue, she decided to take a walk instead. "Maybe I was one of the other types and had been whipping myself for years," she said. Sure enough. She used to see exercise as a lonely endeavor. Now, within ten short minutes of beginning the walk, she felt a new bounce in her step and that lonely feeling took flight. "That horrible fog in my brain lifted, and I am ready to take on life now," she shared. Why, she even had fun!

Determine what you really enjoy, and which time of day is best. Save a few precious minutes each day for precious you. And savor each one. It works.

T: Take the Time to Develop a new Talent

"If I was pain-free, I'd take up tap dancing," Anita told us in class one morning. "It's been my dream for years and years," she went on to say. I was touched by her wistfulness and her honesty. In our writing workshop, I had her explore how she might take those dance lessons in spite of her pain. She came up with some inventive ways to do so.

What would you love to do? Developing a new talent is so freeing. It will take years off your life, a heavy weight from your soul and maybe even pounds from your body. You'll feel lighter, happy, and with more energy than you knew possible. Especially if this is a talent you've longed to develop, a desire you've kept hidden away, for whatever reason : financial, poor self-esteem, I'm too young, too old, I'm not capable, I couldn't really do that, it was just a pipe dream, my spouse would frown on it. Many artists knew from the time they were very young, that they loved to paint. As they grew up and became responsible for finances, they discovered that society didn't reward their creative work financially at all. So they gave up on their dream. I'm here to tell you that you can have it back.

Some young teens and twenty-somethings seem stymied or overwhelmed when asked what they'd like to do with their life. They don't have a clue. It leaves them feeling like there must be something wrong with them. Over the years, I have been amazed at the unlimited variety of professions available. Many can satisfy or incorporate our creative side, leaving us happy and fulfilled, and with a paycheck too. Technical schools abound, thankfully, in our culture now. Electrical courses, automotive, culinary classes, to name just a few, are offered in a venue that doesn't require a college degree. Practical, empowering, they often come with guarantees of a job once the class is successfully completed and requisite exams passed.

Every time I see a movie, and watch the credits rolling by, I am reminded of this. Who knew you could be in clothing design and make movies? What is a key grip? One can write a book, turn it into a screenplay, and then assist in directing the movie. Anything is possible.

So, which talent have you been given, that you've kept secret, have given up on, or told yourself, "I can't do that"? In case you need a memory jogger, here's a list, and you can add many others, I'm sure:

A: Antiques
Archery
Animals...having one, pet-sitting, shelter

B: Bartender
Bicycling
Ballet
Bowling
Baking
Bridge
Bee-keeping

C: Cooking
Chess
Carpentry
Cake Decorating
Candy making
Candles
Canasta
Curling
Carving
Computers
Crochet or knit

D: Dance
Drafting
Deep Sea Fishing
Dominoes
Drumming

E: Education
Entertainment

F: Flowers
Flying
Fishing
Flies, tying

G: Graphic Arts
Gardening
Golf
Gym

H: Hiking
House-sitting
Hot Air ballooning

I: Interior Decorating

J: Jogging
Jamming

K: Karate
Kick Boxing
Knitting
Karaoke
Kites

L: Laughter
Leatherwork
Literacy
Languages

M: Massage
Mechanic
Make-up
Music
Mountain biking
Mountain Climbing
Medicine
Movies
Monopoly

N: Nails
News
Nanny

O: Ombudsman
Outdoor

P: Painting
Pencil Art
Plumbing
Pottery
Photography
Parachuting
Play writing

Q: Quests in nature- lead them, take them
Quilting

R: Radio / CB
Reading to the blind
Reporting
Reading, just for you

S: School
Singing
Sewing
Skiing-downhill
     - Cross-country
Scuba
Screenwriting
Sculpting
Skating- roller blade, ice, roller skating

Swim
T: Tap dance
Theater
Tatting
Tennis
Tole painting
Travel /travel agent
Tai chi
Teach
U: Upholstery
Underwater
V: Veterinarian assistant
Vets, military
Volunteer work
W: Welding
Writing
Whittling
Wine
X: X-ray technician
Radiologist
Y: Yoga
Z: Zoo keeper
Zoology

Pick one and remember you aren't doing this to be an expert in your field, or perfect at it. The playing field is wide open. It is possible to love what you do. There is no one to say that you can't.

What if you could spend the rest of your life being happy and fulfilled because you finally got to choose what you'll do for a "living?" So, what will it be?

U is for Umbrella

When I was a young lass, about twelve years old, leading into my swoon years, I watched the movie Singin' In The Rain. I was hooked. There was Gene Kelly, hot-stepping it down the street and singing his heart out.

I'm singin' in the rain, just singin' in the rain
What a glorious feeling, I'm happy again.
I walk down the lane, with a happy refrain
Just singin', just singin' in the rain.

I remember watching him dance along with his umbrella, getting soaked, and I felt amazement that anyone could actually be happy when it was pouring buckets outside. Because rain to me meant that we couldn't go out to play. Until that day, that is. After being enchanted with that movie and soaking up its message, life was never the same. An umbrella and gumboots were in.

Later on in my years, I realized that Donald O'Connor and Gene Kelly were conveying the theme that we could sing and dance our way through all sorts of emotional rain, if we but chose to. And those tenets of a happy attitude were echoed in the song of Irving Kahal, Francis Wheeler and Sammy Fain, who told us to "Let a smile be your umbrella on a rainy, rainy day." I certainly do not propose that we gloss over every traumatic event in our lives and pretend it didn't happen. It does help, however, to have an armful of cover to keep us warm and dry.

There are all sorts of "umbrellas" we can carry with us on our life's journey:

First, we all have inner strength. Sometimes we have to dig deep to discover ours. This usually occurs in the midst of a huge deluge, downpour or hurricane in our life, but reach deep we can and must.

Picture this:

My friend, MaryLee, decided one blistery hot day, as she was driving in the New Mexico countryside, that the water in a reservoir she had just passed was too enticing to resist. She was miles from any civilization, there were no other cars on the road, and so she pulled over, stripped off all her clothes, climbed up the rickety ladder, and slipped into the cool water. She swam and swam, then turned onto her back and floated along, staring at cloud patterns in the sky, until she was totally relaxed and refreshed.

She realized that she'd better get back on the road, so swam over to the side of the huge metal structure and took hold of the ladder to climb out. To her dismay, it broke off in her hands, and all she could see was a tiny piece of one rung, still stuck on the rim, way above her head. She jumped again and again; she tried to shimmy up the side, all to no avail. The metal was slippery and there was no way to gain a foothold. Over and over she tried until she became exhausted. She realized at this point, that she might die out there, in the blazing sun, all alone.

Suddenly she remembered a story that she'd heard about a frog, who, when stuck in a similar vat, only his was full of milk, never gave up on his attempt to get out. His mate lost hope and drowned. But our courageous frog decided to just keep swimming. Round and round in that milk he swam, his little legs flailing. Pretty soon, he had churned that milk into butter and was able to climb out of the vat to freedom.

MaryLee stopped her sobbing and told herself sternly, if that frog can save himself, so can I. I am not going to die alone out here, naked, in the middle of this desolation. She gathered up all her strength and hurled herself up to the rim of that ten thousand gallon structure, and was able to grab that one tiny piece of the wooden ladder with one hand. She took a huge breath and a mighty heave, and was finally able to pull herself up and out to safety.

Besides learning a valuable lesson about her foolhardy decision to swim there that day, MaryLee discovered her own inner strength and courage. That experience has been her umbrella on other rainy days in her life, ever since.

We must allow ourselves room to fail and have it be perfectly OK. Sly Stallone, in a recent interview with James Tipton, said he purposely chooses activities to explore where he feels a mite uncomfortable. He has to stretch a little so he can expand who he is, not just as an actor, but as a person. Then he gives himself permission for that venture to fall through. In the process, he related, he's learned a whole lot; he's discovered if the venture, relationship or new role is for him. And moreover, with his 'it's all right to fail' umbrella open, he doesn't have to beat himself up but can remain upbeat about the whole experience. I learned a lot from listening to that interview.

The "safe haven" umbrella may be a sunny corner with an easy chair, waiting for you to curl up in; your car, that can take you on short getaway trips, transport you reliably to and fro; a favorite coffee haunt; a painting; music to get lost in; your garden; a special tree in the woods; a rock at the top of the mountain where you hike; your work. I could go on and on. Find what's your safe haven and go there.

The final umbrella is a trusted friend. Someone who is happy by nature. A buddy with whom you can share innermost secrets and know you won't be judged. A friend who will listen when you need it most and who trusts you enough to hear their voice. (It works both ways.) Someone with whom you can giggle hysterically and tell naughty secrets. In Umbrella times, you need a bright, colorful shelter, sturdy, reliable and enduring.

Choose your friend umbrella wisely. You don't need one that is full of holes, overwhelms you with their storms or blows away when you need it most. Carry an umbrella within or close at hand, and you will be able to dance through life's raindrops.

V is For Vacation

"How long has it been, Tony?" I asked my sixty-year-old patient.

"How long for what?" he retorted, eyebrows raised.

"When did you last take a vacation?" I continued, unfazed by his demeanor.

Tony was 'a shaker and a mover.' Always on the go, salesman extraordinaire, worked at least seventy hours a week. The only time he took off was when he went to church on Sunday. For his family's sake, he'd tell you. (And maybe to make new contacts, who knows?)

He was president of the Chamber of Commerce, on the school board, and headed up the committee for the new hospital development.

Why he hadn't had a heart attack yet, I didn't know.

He had come in to the office appointment with headaches, a constant ache at the back of his neck, worse at night when he was resting. I had ordered a battery of tests on him, since this was his only visit in the last ten years. Basically he'd been badgered into my office by his wife and kids, so I did as much as possible while he was agreeable. On examining him, I noted that he had high blood pressure, very aptly named in his case, as 'hypertension.' Tense he was and hyper too.

Now, at my question about vacations, he sat up straight in his chair and shrugged his shoulders, "Hell, Doc, I don't know, it's probably been five years. I haven't had time to go anywhere."

"You haven't *taken* the time to go anywhere," I challenged him.

"Yeah, that's right. I've been too busy, between my job, and committees and all."

"Well, you need to do just that," I said, pulling out my prescription pad. "You know, you can take off for three days and have a totally rejuvenating time, if you choose to. A mini-vacation can be just as rewarding as a longer one. Unwind, refresh, and spend some time with your wife. And it doesn't take a whole lot of planning."

Tony just looked at me and frowned. "You're right Doc, I guess sometimes I forget."

"Well, I'm going to give you the prescription and you'd better follow it! The best medicine for your blood pressure too." I winked at him.

On the prescription was written:

Get a babysitter.
Take three days off.
You and Emily go to Sedona.
Walk every day.

He gazed at it. "That's all?" he asked, incredulous.

"Yes. That's it. You don't need medication right now, you need to get away from the rat race. Slow your pace a little. Come back and see me a week after your trip."

Two weeks later, I walked in to the exam room and there sat Tony, a big grin on his face. His blood pressure had dropped fifteen points, he had lost six pounds and he looked great.

"You were so right, Doc!" A huge smile had replaced the deep furrows on his forehead. "I didn't think that a short trip like that would do me so much good. My wife enjoyed it too. We walked every day, sat around and read, went to some fantastic restaurants, and talked like we haven't done for ages. I didn't realize I was killing myself and her too. She never got to have much fun before this either. I was just being a good provider, or thought I was," he said. "I have to tell ya, I was having chest pains and you know, I bet it was all that stress with no time off."

As he turned to leave, and after we scheduled an appointment to be sure his heart was fine, he turned to me. "Hey, do you think you could give me another prescription like that last one? My partners will never believe me when I tell them I need to take another trip next month."

"Gladly," I told him and pulled out pen and pad. "It'll make you much better at your job when you are at work, more productive. Tell them that, if they haven't noticed already. You'll be running on all eight cylinders instead of trying to do it on four with an empty fuel tank!"

"See you in three months, Doc," he said and departed with a grin.

Tony had thankfully learned the importance of even a mini-vacation. Time away increases your energy and allows you to take a look at situations in your life from a different perspective. Restores your Self and your soul, refreshes relationships and provides for some much-needed rest or exercise.

Be sure to take a time-off trip, not a working one.

If you do have the leisure time and the finances, allow yourself the luxury of a longer trip. The results may be even more dramatic, as with another patient, Bryan. He was becoming very depressed and wondered if he could hold out in his current profession. He owned his own salon, and the pressures were so overwhelming him that he was considering changing jobs altogether. Fortunately, he decided to take a vacation to his homeland of Vietnam. His wife and children had already had their time off, traveling to the Orient the year before while he stayed behind to run the business. Now after seven years with no time off, it was Bryan's turn. He was leaving for a month.

I applauded his decision and told him so. September came and went, everyone survived without him, and the business did well. One day, Bryan bounced into the salon, tanned, vibrant, and grinning. As he polished my nails, he related tales of his reunion with his family, how his mother broke into tears when she saw him; his journeys to the countryside where he had grown up. The time had been rewarding, on many levels. He no longer wanted to sell the business, he had come up with some new ideas to promote it and he had decided to hire an assistant.

When I saw him in October, he was like a new person. "I am new, in every respect. Tell all your friends and patients to take a trip." he said. "When was your last vacation, Dr.? You look like you could use one," he chided.

I laughed, "Yes, I'm sure I could. Good recommendation, Dr. Bryan!"

Remember, a refreshed, renewed heart is much lighter than a tired, congested one, and so are you!

W is for Wow!

Ever been around four-year-olds? Do you remember their fascination with even the smallest details or items? Bugs scooting along in the garden; rain running down the windows; your bright blue eyes or long eyelashes; endless questions: What's in there? Who's that? Why does that cat have stripes? My puppy doesn't. Children are in a perpetual state of amazement at life's endless variety. They don't even have to be persuaded to be there. They just are.

"Where are you from?" we often ask, on meeting a new acquaintance. I'd love to reply, "I live in the state of WOW." I don't say that but remind myself often to be of that essence, have that attitude about life. This wow-ness is fun, it's contagious and I need it to balance the serious, responsible adult lurking inside me, ready to remind me of what I "should" be doing.

If you're this far in the book, you've read many Rx's already. They are suggestions, of course. Perhaps if you are unable to garner up the WOW attitude right now in your life, you'd consider the possibility of being willing to look at it as a new aspect of you. The willingness is of such importance. That in itself is a life-changing step of faith.

This state is where I want to be most of the time. Sometimes, we have gone through traumatic periods, losses in our life that leave us feeling hopeless, helpless or hurt, and nothing seems interesting or fascinating. Well, I am here to tell you that there is a huge world out there just waiting for you to show up again. It is eager to show you its wonders, to enchant you, engage you, take you back to that state of energy known as awe and wonder.

Again from my youth, memories of my parents serve as examples for clarity. My father, Fred, was a meat-and-potatoes guy. After a hearty dinner of roast beef, veggies and mashed potatoes, he'd slowly unwind the wrapper around a loaf of white bread, pull out a slice or two, and then ask us to pass the gravy. We knew what was coming next and Mom was always prepared. Dad would pour the gravy onto his plate, and then dip his bread in it, soaking it through and through. He'd cut it up with knife and fork, and then thoroughly enjoy every morsel, cleaning his plate like a starving pooch, with the last forkful.

In my church group, we had a fundraiser one Friday night where we were introduced to tacos. This was Vancouver, Canada, it was the late 1950's, and tacos were the newest craze, another experience to rave about.

A few days later, I was in charge of making dinner for our family. I decided to initiate them into the world of tacos, salsa and refried beans. Carefully I chopped up tomatoes, shredded lettuce, sautéed the hamburger, and bought the taco shells from our corner grocery store. I was so enthused that I didn't mind walking the eight blocks to the store and back.

I remember to this day my father's comments and reaction to that entrée. His behavior at that white enameled kitchen table was worthy of an Oscar nomination.

"How are we supposed to eat these damn things?" he'd demanded.

"Like this, Dad!" as I demonstrated this new skill. My brothers loved them. My mother tolerated them. Dad's comment was, "Well, they're OK if you like eating stale book covers."

I didn't dare ask him how he'd ever come to eat book covers, but I got the picture.

Nonetheless, this was a huge step for my dad. It paved the way for forays into Chinese food. It gave Mom a chance to slowly introduce other foods into what had become a humdrum menu for her. Dad had been willing (albeit reluctantly) to look at the possibility of there being more to the evening meal than Billie Beef on his plate, disguised as hamburger, pot roast, meat loaf, chili, stew or just plain old steak. I don't think he'd attempted to cook any meal over their many years together, except for salmon on the BBQ when we were at our summer cabin.

When my two brothers and I were very young, Dad did cook scrambled eggs one Sunday morning, as we were hungry and Mom was ill. The only problem was that he had the bright idea of putting honey in them. Honey? In scrambled eggs? We kids raised a ruckus and turned up our little noses at his creation. That may have had something to do with him never attempting anything with a spoon and frying pan ever since.

My brother and sister-in-law, Murray and Carel, gifted my parents with a Chinese cooking course one Christmas. Dad and Mom cooked together one night a week with an Oriental chef, where they ended up chopping vegetables into small pieces, sautéed meat, and created delicious sauces. They loved it! Dad's creative skills sprang into action and gave him many wonder-filled, happy moments. He definitely shifted his attitude and because of his willingness to look at himself and his habits, experienced wonder on a regular basis. And Mom was very happy to share the kitchen duties. When I'd fly home for visits, it made my heart sing to see and hear him in the kitchen, whistling happily while tempting foods sizzled in the wok and chopsticks flew.

Once we open up enough in one area, it seems that other aspects of our lives can be freed too. We can find that willingness to allow new, awesome happenings will reveal many worlds of pleasure. Be as little children, a wise man once said. Try it and you will find he was right. Lightheartedness will reign. WOW!

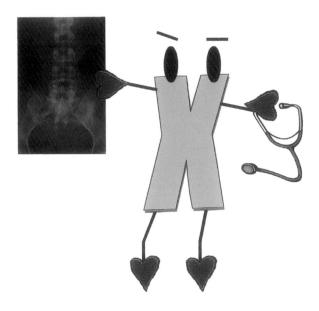

X is for X-ray

What do X-rays do?

1. They see what may not be obvious superficially.
2. They can be directed to focus in on a specific area.
3. They can pick up small details that we may not have seen in the "bigger picture" or that may be masked by our positive attitude, flush of a new love, accommodation or cover-up that is entirely unconscious.
4. X-rays can point out areas of abnormality or spots that may give us difficulty or disease later on.

When I was a child, I had long feet, very long feet. My grandmother, staring one day at my shoes as she helped me finish dressing, mentioned the fact to me.

"Yes, Nana," I'd replied with my five-year-old innate wisdom. "If I didn't have such long feet, I'd fall over!"

My parents took me to a shoe store, where the salesman carefully measured my feet. I remember him pressing on the top of the shoe and I would have to wiggle my toes inside. Then, he had me stand inside the "magic machine." There, an X-ray picture would show if there was enough room inside that shoe for my bones to grow. Of course, I am showing my age as I relate this experience, for these machines were outlawed once we knew of the dangers of repeated radiation.

However, in those days, they always made shoe-buying a happy, exciting endeavor. By the time we left the shoe department, my parents knew this was the perfect fit; I had a beautiful new pair of shoes, and an adventure besides.

Today we often have no such direct visual evidence of what is perfect for us. We do not see a red flashing siren on our right elbow, warning of impending danger; nor do we possess a Pinocchio nose that grows when others tell us a mistruth or we lie to ourselves. But we do have a very wise "magic machine" inside each one of us. We can look into ourselves and discover the answers to questions:

Do I feel good, or how about great, after I've been with Hank, or Emily (or whatever name you want)?

Am I more lighthearted when I finish my day at XYZ Pharmaceuticals than I am after work at ABC Construction?

What does my inner X-ray reveal to me about the level of my love's delight in me? Am I delighted in them? What flashes on your inner XRay screen in the delight view box?

I love the word 'delight.' It goes one step beyond concepts such as 'relate' or 'enjoy' and way farther than 'put up with' or 'tolerate.' In a class I took, I had a fun Ah-ha moment, when I realized that I could have a relationship in which both partners actually took great delight in the other.

More questions we can ask our higher selves, that inner X-ray:

How does my body feel? Can my bones wriggle about with plenty of room, or do I feel confined; can I breathe easily or do I feel like I have asthma? Are my muscles tied up in knots? How's my energy? Do I feel absolutely exhausted or am I exhilarated after an evening with that person?

Do I feel excited, challenged, and enthralled? Is my mind at ease, or am I all stressed out?

Am I spiritually at peace, content with the decision I just made?

Are my emotions in chaos or sailing along on a smooth course?

All of these puzzles can be answered if we develop the habit of looking inside and take the time to ask the pertinent questions. Then more time, just a little when we get really good at this, to hear the answers.

We all have this power available to us. It is in everyone. So use your inner wisdom, your magic machine to confirm if a job, situation or person is the perfect one for you. By all means, make an agreement with yourself to honestly ask the question and then heed the results you get. Be willing to see the big picture. Be authentic about what you see for yourself. You will be lighthearted.

Y is for Yes

You sit in the doctor's exam room. He or she scans your chart, the latest blood test results; wraps the blood pressure cuff around your arm, takes note of your weight. As the little needle on the cuff falls, they squiggle some mysterious lines in your chart. You strain to read upside-down. Even if you could decipher it, none of it would make much sense.

Suddenly, all two hundred and fifty pounds of them turn in their chair and utter those horrible words, "You have to exercise, Mrs. Pleasantly Plump."

Oh, brother, for this I came to see the doctor? you mutter to yourself. "Yes, yes, I promise, Dr. I will start tomorrow. In fact I already have an appointment at the gym."

Makes you nauseated, doesn't it? *Why can't they just give me a pill? That will take care of it.*
HA!

We must say yes to what we know is right for us, for our emotional as well as our physical body. Until we know on a very deep level that we want to move our bodies, we're going to feel like victims. At the mercy of someone else's grand idea of what is right for us, we'll feel like we are being dictated to, instead of us being in charge.

We are not going to comply until we throw ourselves 100% into agreement, every cell and molecule saying Yes. We have to make those prescriptions our truth.

So, instead of buying into the Dr's words of wisdom, we say:

"I just don't have the time. I am too busy."

"What do they know? They are overweight themselves. They'd better practice what they preach."

"When am I supposed to fit that into my day? Are you going to do my laundry, look after three kids and cook the meals?"

"I hate walking." Or swimming, yoga, jogging, gym, baseball, tennis, etc.

(No kidding, once I had a patient who argued with every single activity they or I thought up.)

"It's too boring. I could never do that."

"I could never go to the gym looking like this! I'd be totally embarrassed." (You mean you don't feel that way in the grocery store?)

"I've tried it before. It doesn't work."

"My friend dropped dead when they were jogging. I don't want that to happen to me."

"What in the heck does my physical health have to do with my emotions or depression, anyway?"

Or how about: "I am so tired. I don't have enough energy to go for a walk."

But when we take charge, suddenly we become masters of our fate. We say Yes, way deep down and it becomes easy. We become the 'dictators of', instead of being 'dictated to.'

Very quickly, we begin to feel more energetic, stronger, less stressed. We can stop ourselves before we snap at our spouse or kids. After about three weeks, sometimes sooner, we realize we actually want to get out and move our bodies. It becomes a driving force within us because we feel so much better on all levels. Our bodies are pumping out those prostaglandins, antidepressant hormones, and immune builders. As we walk along, we sing with James Brown, "I feel go-o-od!" Those knees that bothered us so much a few weeks earlier now carry us around the court quite easily, thank you.

Mr. Jamieson was a seventy-year-old man in my practice who had come for a visit because of horrible aching pain in both legs. After examination and testing, we discovered he had marked narrowing of the arteries that carry blood to his legs and feet. His type of blockage was not in one place, which would have made it treatable by surgery. Rather, it was more extensive and carried down even to the smaller arteries.

Mr. Jamieson tried to walk but the pain would stop him each time. He would have to sit down, even on the curb, wait for the squeezing pressure in his legs to stop, and then continue on his walk. But he persisted. "I just have to walk through the pain, Dr. But the neat thing is, I can go a bit further each week. I think it's working."

By the end of three months, Mr. Jamieson had shed ten pounds, had more energy, but best of all, his excruciating leg pains were gone. By the end of six months, his body had built new networks of arterioles, which we could document on his vascular studies.

Our bodies truly are amazing. If we listen to them and work in sync with what they tell us, we too can experience pain relief, more vitality, better sleep and increased muscular strength. We can own a whole new outlook on life.

Say Yes to moving your body.

It's also important to align with foods that that are best for us. I have come to the conclusion after seeing thousands of overweight patients in the last thirty years that this arena too is about balance. Remember how, for years, we focused on low-fat diets? Many folks, if they adhered to this plan and their exercise regime, would lose weight. But for about twenty-five percent, no matter how hard they tried, their pounds stuck to them like glue. Then along came the low carbohydrate diets, hundreds of them. Same results. Many people lost pounds, others couldn't toss off one.

Some of us eat way too many fats while others devour over eighty percent carbs in our meals. So if we are the high carb eaters, a low fat diet won't help us much at all. Likewise, a low carb diet will cause no results for an individual who inhales fried fish, cheese and other greasy foods. The main thing is to create balance in the foods we eat, drink lots of water to flush out the byproducts of our increased metabolism and establish a faithful, consistent exercise program.

I want to say one thing about sugar and that is this: if you eat a lot of high-sugar foods, you'll be depressed. No two ways about it. Sugar is one of the most addicting substances with which we assault our bodies. Because it is a food, we can easily overlook its addictive potential. If you are a chocoholic or pasta junkie, read the book entitled "Sugar Blues." It is an excellent eye-opener. Follow what it says and you will be a happy individual. Of course, if there are emotional challenges in the way, take care of those too. At one point in my career, I hired a hypnotherapist to assist with my weight-loss patients. She ended up doing a lot of counseling, as well as hypnosis. As patients came to trust us, they were able to look at the emotional cause of their weight gain. Then they were able to participate fully in the physical aspects of the program, and the pounds began to fall off and stay off.

Take a good honest look at yourself, love and honor who you are and say Yes. Yes to eating what's best for you. Yes to moving your body. Your emotions, spirit and mental side will lighten up too.

Z is for Zebra

Z is for Zebra
My striped friend.
I see you and wonder
Do your stripes ever end?

Are you white over black
Or charcoal on white?
Rigid beliefs of you
Transform in new light.

A fresh way of seeing
A joyous one too
I never thought life's lessons
Would be learned in a zoo.

A bright way of being
I've learned in these pages
For lighthearted living
Can remain through my ages.

That's nothing to scoff at
For I've learned much herein
That laughter is healing
Face each day with a grin.

Yes, Z is for Zebra
Your stripes are your friend.
Where do **yours** start
And when do they end?

Dare you throw them right off?
What then will you be?
Try running naked with giggles
From A through to Z.

For those of you reading
Be you damsel or dude,
Your best dress in life
Is a great attitude.
Bless you.

If any of you have similar inspiring miracle stories to share, please write me at my website. I would love to hear from you!

My email address is: mmears@cox.net and website is www.outskirtspress.com/ABCsLight heartedLiving

Printed in the United States
124376LV00004BB